The Art of Saying Yes To U With No F*cks Given

Uncompromised Fulfillment: Embracing Your True Path.

Deva Pink

Deva Pink
The Art of Saying Yes To U With No F*cks Given

Published by BooxAI
ISBN: 978-965-578-776-4

This book is wholeheartedly dedicated to each individual I've had the privilege of encountering, with a special emphasis on those cherished souls closest to my heart. The invaluable lessons of my journey are a testament to your profound impact on my life.

Table Of Contents

Chapter Six

About the Author

Deva Pink, a force to be reckoned with, hails from the vibrant streets of Brooklyn, New York. Born into a world where Arabic was her first language, she embarked on a journey that would make her a household name, an inspirational life coach, and a hairstylist to the stars.

As the loving mother of two, a daughter and a son, Deva Pink understands the importance of balancing a thriving career with family life. Her remarkable career as a hairstylist has taken her into the glitzy world of celebrities, film, and television. However, it was her unwavering dedication to the everyday working woman that became the cornerstone of her illustrious career.

Deva's artistic touch graced the sets of major films, including the groundbreaking "Black Panther 2" and television shows like "Swarm" on Amazon Prime. Her hairstyling prowess even made its way to the cover of Rolling Stone magazine, where she styled the hair of the iconic Kat Graham.

Yet, Deva Pink's passion extends far beyond hairstyling. She's a life coach with a vision, driven by the dream of inspiring women and humanity as a whole to rediscover self-love and courageously prioritize themselves. In early 2023, she took a significant step toward this vision by releasing her first book, "Hey Girl Hey Say Yes to U," a guide filled with powerful tools for self-discovery, which quickly found its way into homes worldwide.

And now, with boundless enthusiasm, Deva Pink proudly presents her second masterpiece, "The Art of Saying Yes to U with no fucks given." In this book, she fearlessly explores the art of unapologetically embracing one's true self, empowering individuals to live life on their terms, free from the constraints of societal judgment.

Deva Pink's life story, her unwavering commitment to uplifting others, and her unique perspective on self-love make her a beacon of inspiration for all who seek to say "yes" to themselves, with no fucks given.

Website: www.devapink.com
Instagram: @Iamdevapink

Introduction

We all want change, right? But let's admit it: making it happen isn't always a walk in the park. We humans are kind of wired to dodge anything that might bring us discomfort or disappointment. But here's the real deal: none of us get out of this life without a few bumps and bruises, and, well, we're not getting out of here alive either!

So, here's the thing with the whole Say Yes to U journey: it's about facing the fact that life doesn't always dish out what we're hoping for. If we're not content with a little, guess what? Even a lot won't cut it. If we're not okay with that place we're at right now, we'll never find contentment or real fulfillment anywhere down the road. Life isn't a piece of cake. This journey is a tough cookie. It's like climbing a mountain: You need to put in the effort, train hard, and sure, it won't be easy, but there's no magic solution, instant transformation, or quick fix. Like my mom used to say: *Change doesn't happen overnight, but the desire for change can start right now.* That desire is what's going to make you dig deep into your soul. Change isn't something forced upon you. It's a choice you make. You can totally stick to your current path and no one will make you budge an inch. Your personal growth journey is like a fine recipe: Begin only when you're genuinely ready and it feels like the right move for you. Your time is precious, so invest it where it matters most: in you. Trust me, I've been there and I get how intimidating this journey can be right at the start.

But, hey, you always have a choice: answer that inner call or just let it slide by. This journey of self-discovery and authentic living is not a sprint. However, it's more like a sequence of phases that need a whole lot of patience and faith. It's tempting to speed through life like a binge-watcher, wanting quick fixes and instant results, but true transformation isn't some rapid event. It's about soaking up knowledge and growing understanding that everything is a process. Embracing and trusting your personal evolution is crucial. And let me tell you, that fear of pain can often stand tall as a major challenge in your path to transformation. Sometimes it's so scary that we end up causing ourselves even more pain while avoiding it. It's funny how what we try to dodge becomes our reality. We've been wired to see pain as this big negative, but what if it's just an essential part of our growth story?

Consider this book as a compass, a guidepost and the Pink Print for those searching for self-discovery, healing, personal growth and the courage to say yes to themselves unapologetically!

It's like a roadmap that'll help you navigate life's twists and turns, shedding light on those signals and wisdom that might have slipped through the cracks. Through introspection and the courage to confront that buried pain, you'll embark on a profound journey toward embracing your true self. Saying yes to yourself, taking this plunge into self-discovery, doesn't just open doors: it's like opening a whole new universe of possibilities. Well, change it's a given, right? However, when you actively take part in your own healing and growth, you're not just going with the flow, but steering your ship. You're shaping the course and outcomes of your life, one transformative step at a time.

CHAPTER ONE

No F*cks – Accept It

There is a time in our lives when we reach a breaking point, a moment where the idea of adopting an *I don't give a F*ck* attitude can seem both liberating and terrifying. It's like standing at the edge of a cliff, unsure whether to take the plunge or step back. You start questioning the very purpose of everything you've been doing.

Imagine if everything you thought you knew, believed in and held onto suddenly crumbled away like a sandcastle, washed away by the tide. The solid ground you thought you were standing on becomes shaky, leaving you struggling to balance. It's like sinking in quicksand, slowly getting pulled into.

Life is like a river, constantly moving and changing. To truly experience its flow, we must let go of the riverbank. Letting go becomes an act of trust in life's journey, a way of embracing who we are. We finally understand the joy of riding life's waves in this letting go. As change propels us forward, releasing our grip and allowing life to guide us becomes an act of courage. When we embrace the rhythm of the unknown, we free ourselves from the illusion of control. But what happens when we can't let go? When we cling to our fears, we chain ourselves to a life dominated by those fears. We invest our time and energy in things that don't truly matter. Living defensively becomes our norm, keeping us constantly on guard and fearful of what might happen. This kind of life can feel like an endless void, no matter how much we try to fill it.

For example, a woman unexpectedly fell head over heels in love with a man. They shared almost every waking moment for a remarkable decade, seamlessly blending their lives. Of course, they had their fair share of minor and major disagreements, but their bond remained unbreakable. Laughter, genuine friendship and adventure were the cornerstones of their relationship, making it almost addictive in its magic. Despite their beauty, an undercurrent of uncertainty began to sneak in. This woman, hoping for a fairy tale ending, silently wondered whether this love story would follow the script she had envisioned or plummet into another heartbreak. This inner conflict casts a shadow over her happiness, causing her to doubt herself within the relationship she cherished. She started looking for signs and clues that could foretell the future.

Desperate for answers, she unknowingly fueled the very fear she sought to avoid. In her attempt to prevent a potential breakup, she inadvertently sowed the seeds of destruction.

This fear-driven expectation grew into a monstrous force, leading her to undermine the very love she was trying to protect subconsciously. Terrified of losing the man she deemed her soulmate, she inadvertently set off a chain reaction that would eventually end their story. The fear of the unknown swallowed her, turning their once beautiful relationship into a roller coaster of anxiety and doubt. The ride ended and with it, the relationship concluded what she had dreaded: another failed relationship.

This small story illustrates the power of expectations and how they can grow silently and shape our reality. Fueled by fear and uncertainty, they can transform the most beautiful connections into self-fulfilling prophecies. Holding onto expectations too tightly can sometimes drive the outcome we fear the most.

Fear and expectations have a cunning way of sneaking into our lives, stealing away the potential for fulfillment and replacing it with a life consumed by apprehension and anxiety. It's often said that we fear what we attract, suggesting that fear holds the uncanny ability to materialize chaos in our lives, as if fear alone possesses the power to wreak havoc, even without invitation. But what if we pause and examine this thought more closely? In my view, fear is not merely an isolated force; it's intricately woven into the very fabric of our being. It's a thread that runs deep, shaping our behaviors and decisions more than we realize. Often, its presence is so discreet that we remain oblivious to its influence. We might find ourselves pointing fingers at others when things go awry, conveniently passing the blame onto them for not meeting our expectations.

We unwittingly bestow upon them the immense responsibility of fulfilling our desires and subsequently, our behavior becomes entangled in this complex web of anticipation and blame. We may even find ourselves blaming life itself, questioning the universe's integrity, or challenging a higher power's credibility when our expected outcomes fall short. The paradox lies in our tendency to assign blame externally while failing to recognize how our fears and expectations shape our reality.

The truth is both fear and expectations are intertwined in the roots of our existence. They dictate our actions, mold our perspectives and ultimately determine our experiences.

Instead of simply attributing all mishaps to external factors, maybe it's time to dig deeper, acknowledging the potent force that fears and expectations exert within us. This awareness could be the key to unlocking a more authentic and fulfilling life. In our contemporary world, expectations often sprout from thin air, rarely finding their roots in the solid ground of reality.

As these expectations take hold, they tend to summon fear, subtly pushing us onto a defensive stance.

A telling example is the prevailing sensitivity surrounding virtually any topic today. Once celebrated, the concept of free speech now tiptoes on eggshells, wary of ruffling feathers and triggering retaliatory reactions. We've become a society primed for defense, ready to assert our rights even if it means being wrong in another sense.

This phenomenon mirrors the outcome of living a life woven with fear, bristling with defense mechanisms and weighed down by the burden of expectations. It's as though every facet of existence transforms into a battleground of dichotomies, where is right versus wrong, blame versus innocence. This reflexive mindset extends to many issues: assigning blame for personal failings in love, happiness, success, and also, demanding solutions to global crises like hunger, drugs and homelessness. Yet, paradoxically, this insistence on defining problems might be the core problem itself. Could our fixation on imaginary expectations close our eyes to the essence of life as it unfolds before us? Do we struggle to embrace the present moment's reality because we are fixated on a future that aligns with our preconceived visions? The discomfort arises when life, true to its nature, doesn't comply with our scripted version of events. In this complex interplay, it's essential to understand that life, like the certainty of death, is marked by a series of variables intermingling with our existence. We must acknowledge our role in how these variables take shape and our influence on the lens through which we perceive them. This web of variables, driven by the gift of free will, offers us an abundance of choices, opportunities, changes and transformations.

The journey paved with expectations and fantasies often makes us feel trapped and disheartened. It's as if we're caught in a loop, fixating solely on our hopes and desires, believing that their fulfillment is the key to defining our existence. Unfortunately, this approach often ushers in an array of unwelcome emotions, like pain, heartache, disappointment and even fear. Expectations, those vivid mental pictures we paint, often become like stubborn glue, adhering us to a version of reality we're reluctant to release. Sometimes, we attempt to edit or adapt these images to fit the ebb and flow of our lives. Yet, these idealized scenarios can easily blur the lines between what's real and merely a product of our imagination. Perhaps that's why the saying "ignorance is bliss" holds some truth and why the allure of fantasy can occasionally outshine reality. The idea of living in a world untainted by the weight of expectations and the harsh realities they often bring.

In the tale of our lives, we often wrestle with the conflict between what we want to happen and what unfolds. It's as if we're woven into a narrative that oscillates between dreams, fantasies and the harshness of reality. The challenge lies in finding the balance – a dance between the two realms that allows us to hold onto our desires while remaining grounded in the present moment.

Expectations act as a web that entangles our ability to accept life as it is. We clutch onto our desires, hoping they will flawlessly fit into the story we've scripted, a tale one of unending happiness, prosperity and security. It's as if we've coated life in excess sweetness, forgetting that a balanced blend is far healthier than an overload of sugary dreams, but that's just the surface. Reality paints a different picture. Our work-places, schools, homes and relationships often become canvases for our unrealistic expectations. We find ourselves caught in a silent struggle to uphold these ideals with grace, an exhausting endeavor that often leaves us feeling trapped – as if we're living "as if" rather than authentically being. The irony is that not only do our expectations imprison those around us, but they also lock us in a cell of our own making. We construct this prison with our own hands, crafting bars from the very beliefs we hold dear. It's fascinating that many of these expectations are designed to be self-fulfilling prophecies. We shape our lives according to what we anticipate, even when those predictions are just figments of our imagination.

That's where acceptance comes in, being a precious key to unlock the mysteries that confront us. It's a deceptively simple concept, yet it can feel immensely complex to practice. Acceptance doesn't mean we toss aside our dreams and aspirations, leaving them by the wayside like forgotten relics. Instead, it urges us to become discerning. What truly matters? What holds genuine value in our lives? Perhaps we find ourselves tangled in the belief that only one true love is destined for us, a notion that may have inadvertently fueled the desire to cling to that fantasy. Yet, here's the truth: it's okay for fantasies to hold value, but they must align with our inner compass. When the story we've envisioned no longer matches the reality we face, accepting that divergence becomes a powerful act. Essentially, it's about allowing our hopes and dreams to evolve, acknowledging that some chapters have reached their end. And yes, acceptance might sound simple in words, but it's far from easy in practice. It's a process that requires peeling back attachment layers and embracing the unknown. It's a journey toward finding peace amidst the tangle of expectations and, ultimately, being okay with the "what is" rather than the "what if."

Embracing acceptance paves the path for the art of "no F's given." As we learn to dial down our expectations and embrace life's realities, a profound truth emerges that first, we must wholly accept ourselves. It's about stepping into our skin unapologetically without needing validation or understanding from others. We share our stories, not seeking approval or rejection, but in our quest to be the best version of ourselves. To be *unapologetic with no F's given* means just that: releasing the grip on unrealistic ideals that promise eternal happiness. Every day we're alive is a gift, a happily ever after of its kind until the final curtain falls. Whose permission are we waiting for to live authentically? Who holds the manual to guide our unique compass? Why do we continue to seek approval for simply being ourselves? The answer lies in the journey of learning, the ebb and flow of creation and destruction that shapes our lives. And in the end, yes, we do leave this earth, but what if the perceived failures of unmet expectations were detours that led us closer to our true, authentic desires? What if the pain of a decade-long love story's end was the catalyst for an unexpected freedom? This newfound freedom is the essence of living life on our terms, unfiltered and without the weight of unnecessary concerns. It's realizing that caring too much and not caring at all don't always offer the solutions we seek. True liberation might come from transcending both states and residing in the neutrality of our emotions. In this space, we become unapologetic, owning our experiences, shedding unnecessary baggage and embracing life's uncertainties without the burden of excessive expectations. So, is there a lesson in all of this? Perhaps it's in recognizing that while fantasies might offer a respite from life's trials, they can also distract us from embracing our reality's genuine beauty and complexity. It's not about discarding our dreams, but rather learning to coexist with them, letting them inspire us while understanding that life is a canvas, both beautiful and messy.

F*ck It — Be Vulnerable

There was a time in my life when I believed I was flourishing. I paid my bills, enjoyed traveling, was in an amazing relationship, dining out and indulged in the vibrant nightlife scene. I would seek solace in alcohol and mild substances, hoping they would provide an external high to match my inner state. It's really interesting trying to find an internal high externally. It's like expecting a clear reflection in a murky pond; what you see on the surface doesn't mirror the depths within. I was convinced that this external picture defined my happiness for a while. Like this magical script, life seemed wonderful, full of blessings and hard-earned achievements, as if the seeds you planted were finally blooming. I decided to live a bicoastal life between LA and Atlanta, thinking it would give me a fresh start and a renewed sense of purpose. So, back in Atlanta, with all my plans and dreams lined up, I was confident that everything was falling perfectly into place. I was hired as one of the stylists at a celebrity high-end salon. My apartment in Dunwoody was pretty cozy and driving around in my "dream car" felt like a tangible symbol of success. I was convinced that I had found my groove, my road to continued happiness.

And then, out of the blue, boom! Life threw me this major curveball that was spinning me in circles. It was like watching a carefully built tower of cards collapse in seconds. Can you imagine feeling like you're on this winning streak and suddenly, you're faced with something that knocks you off your feet? That's how I felt when I was held responsible for a fire that broke out in the salon. It was beyond surreal. The fact that it affected me and the other stylists hit me like a ton of bricks. Suddenly, the thriving workplace we knew was gone and with it went a chunk of our sense of security. As if that wasn't enough, life had yet another surprise in store. My ex-husband, in a surprising twist, reneged on our agreed-upon visitation schedule for the kids. It felt like the universe was piling up challenges and I was left grappling with these overwhelming changes on multiple fronts. It was like standing in the middle of a storm, questioning how things had turned so chaotic so quickly. As I sat on my couch on a rainy day in Atlanta, I felt a deep sense of sadness and disappointment in myself. The fire had triggered a downward spiral of negative emotions and I found myself fixating on everything going wrong in my life. In that moment of introspection, I gazed up at the ceiling and posed a question to myself: *Why am I feeling empty despite seemingly doing everything right?* Surprisingly, a voice within me responded, *It's because you're not saying yes to you.*

This answer baffled me. Was I saying yes to me? I associated that phrase with selfishness, remembering the times I had chosen my needs over those of my friends and family. The concept felt confusing and contradictory. So, I decided to sit with this, allowing it to sink in. Curious, I asked the voice within, "How do I say yes to me?" The response was unexpected: "You must return to a time when you felt this way. Look for similarities in your expectations. Embarking on this journey of self-discovery isn't easy. It involves connecting with our unresolved emotions, making us feel vulnerable and emotionally fragile. I was judgmental of myself for wallowing in self-pity, for feeling like life had consistently let me down. After months of self-reflection, something shifted. It was like my emotional and spiritual self was finally getting a chance to speak, to communicate with my mind and body. I realized that I had been so focused on doing everything right that I ended up on what now seems to be the "wrong" side of the street. The irony of it all.

The day life introduced me to the concept of saying yes to myself was the day my life took a turn. While my life had undergone significant changes before, this time was different. I was fully conscious of the existence of my inner world – tuned in to my internal landscape rather than being preoccupied with external factors. This newfound awareness triggered a potent curiosity about understanding who I truly was. I delved deep into self-exploration, driven by questions like: Why had I survived so long without giving genuine priority and love to myself? Could it be that my past struggles in relationships were somehow tied to this neglect? Perhaps, I realized, I had been living with a kind of blindness, maybe even a fear, preventing me from peering into the abyss of my emotions. It occurred to me that I had constructed a belief that I could conceal my genuine emotions, much like many of us do. We attempt to mask our emotions, because they reside within us, hidden from the external world's view. We assume nobody can discern the truth of our internal battles because their attention is fixated on our external actions and behaviors – the elaborate performances we stage for the world.

Exploring the past can be a sensitive endeavor, especially when our goal is to observe rather than pass judgment on the resurfacing emotions. Emotions are not invisible; they manifest in our actions and behaviors, offering visible glimpses into our internal world. However, what we project outwardly doesn't always mirror what we're experiencing on the inside. The journey begins by asking ourselves the fundamental question: What suppressed emotions or hidden truths am I carrying? But the process doesn't end with asking questions. Instead, it continues by learning to answer them using logic, our senses and from going within. Logic represents the analytical mind, while our sense embodies the wisdom of the heart. Just as Jesus said, merging the two creates unity. This unity symbolizes awareness – recognizing the interplay between the mind and the senses. As long as the mind and the senses remain in isolation, we're bound to struggle to reach the core authenticity within ourselves. The essence of this journey is to bridge the gap between the two, enabling us to embrace our true selves in their entirety.

Imagine life as a puzzle; each piece represents a part of who you are. As you journey through this puzzle, you realize some pieces are hidden beneath layers. Vulnerability is like putting the puzzle pieces together, revealing the grander picture. Think of vulnerability as one of the Pink Print in this intricate puzzle of self-discovery. It's like opening a door to a room within yourself that you didn't fully know existed. Once you become aware of this hidden part, it's as if your true self is patiently waiting for you to acknowledge its presence. Vulnerability isn't about weakness; it's about courage. It's one of the tools that helps you unlock resistance you might not even know is there.

I had taken pride in my perceived emotional strength for a long time. I could easily walk away from people and situations I thought were causing unhappiness. It was my way of protecting myself, but the irony is, how often can we keep walking away only to find ourselves repeatedly in similar situations? That's where vulnerability steps in. It's like slowly peeling away the layers of a protective wall we've built. Each layer we remove feels like a brick taken out of that wall. Sounds simple, right? In reality, it's challenging. None of us want to admit that we've been wearing a mask of strength to the world while inside. We've been grappling with emotions like hurt and disappointment.

Facing this truth can feel like exposing ourselves as a fraud. We've been projecting an image of emotional strength for so long that we forget we can have real feelings. It's like admitting that we've been pretending to be okay when, in reality, we're human and we have our ups and downs. This journey is about peeling away those emotional layers, acknowledging that vulnerability isn't a sign of weakness, but rather an act of courage. It's a means of welcoming your genuine self, embracing all emotions, and taking a stride toward comprehending your essence and the reasons behind your decisions. Vulnerability can feel like walking on a tightrope without a safety net. It's tough to reveal that we have emotions and care, especially when we've spent so long denying ourselves the chance to express our true emotions. We've become experts at hiding our feelings and showing a tough exterior to the world. This façade of strength can lead others to assume we don't need emotional connection. We've been through a lot of pain and disappointment to shield ourselves from more hurt, we've built emotional walls. Ironically, these walls meant to protect us end up isolating us from others and ourselves. We're left feeling an aching emptiness. So, we wear a mask of indifference, portraying ourselves as people who don't care. Remember the saying: "Sticks and stones may break my bones, but words will never hurt"? Well, sometimes words do hurt. Each of us has been affected by hurtful words at some point. Growing up, I was teased for having big lips. Those words stuck and I began to despise that part of me. I even hated my smile, because I believed the criticism that my big lips were ugly. Those hurtful words piled up inside me over the years and the worst part was that I started to echo those negative words to myself. We walk through life trying to be strong, acting like negative words don't affect us. We don the armor of confidence, but deep down, we still carry the weight of those hurtful words, and the truth is, they do affect us. They shape how we see ourselves, carry ourselves and interact with the world. We're carrying a heavy backpack of hurtful words, trying to march forward as if it's not weighing us down.

The vulnerability involves recognizing this burden and starting to unload it. It's admitting that those words hurt and that we're human, not invincible. It's allowing ourselves to acknowledge the pain they caused and seeking healing. It's learning to put down that heavy backpack and walk a bit lighter, even one step at a time. Vulnerability becomes the key that unlocks the door to the chambers of our hidden pain and unrealistic expectations. It's like slowly dismantling a wall, brick by brick, and as the bricks come down, we start to feel the emotions trapped behind them. It's through feeling pain that we can truly feel alive, because if we suppress pain, we also dull our ability to experience joy, love and everything in between. When pain is suppressed, it doesn't disappear; it just becomes a heavy weight we carry within. And as strange as it may seem, this weight often translates into expectations from others to heal us, to fill the emptiness we feel. It's a dangerous cycle, seeking love and validation externally to fix an internal wound.

Recognizing this pattern is a breakthrough; vulnerability allows us to confront it head-on. I remember the moment I acknowledged how those words about my appearance had affected me. I let myself feel the hurt and I cried, not just for the present, but for the little girl who carried that pain for years without an outlet. Releasing that emotion was freeing, like unburdening a load I had carried for so long. It was a realization that words have power and acknowledging their impact on us isn't a sign of weakness, but strength. This revelation shifted my perspective, helping me understand that accepting our sensitivity and acknowledging the hurt caused by words is crucial. It's not about letting others dictate our emotions, but acknowledging our feelings. By doing so, we take charge of our emotional well-being, preventing the external world from defining us. This process makes us resilient and able to withstand negative influences without internalizing them. It's a step towards self-love and self-acceptance, which are like shields guarding us from allowing physical or emotional abuse to infiltrate our lives. Vulnerability transforms pain into a source of strength, making us more attuned to ourselves and others, ultimately leading us to a more authentic and fulfilling life journey.

Emotional Pain Killer

I remember the first time Keisha Lonnon introduced me to the term "emotional painkillers." It happened during one of those heart-to-heart talks where I'd spill my frustrations, wrapping up my rant with phrases like "it doesn't matter" or "I don't care." Keisha would calmly point out, "You're using emotional painkillers." Those words caught me off guard. I'd never heard that phrase before, but it instantly intrigued me. Emotional painkillers? What did that even mean? It was as if her words held a secret message, like she was hinting that my responses were somehow a shield against some emotional trigger. Keisha's comment left me curious and motivated to dig deeper into this concept. What did she mean by emotional painkillers and how did they work? As I thought more about it, I slowly grasped its meaning. Emotional painkillers, I realized, were like psychological pain relievers we use to momentarily numb or suppress our emotional distress. They're like self-prescribed remedies, where we convince ourselves that what we're feeling is either real or not genuine or that someone else is the cause of our pain and disappointment. These emotional painkillers shield us from confronting the raw truth of our emotions. They put up a wall between our inner vulnerabilities and our conscious minds, stopping us from fully admitting and dealing with our pain. We create a temporary escape from discomfort by pushing aside our feelings or blaming them on external factors. It's a way of self-defense.

Contemplating the consequences of relying on emotional painkillers, I came to realize that while they might offer momentary relief, they also came with a price. Yes, they provided a quick fix, but hindered our progress and recovery. By avoiding confrontation with our emotions, we robbed ourselves of the chance to deal with the core issues causing our pain. We kept ourselves in a loop of evasion, never truly resolving the underlying problems that desperately needed our attention.

Understanding how emotional painkillers play out in our own lives can be both eye-opening and demanding. It meant confronting our tendencies to shield ourselves and admitting when we used these tactics to numb our feelings.

Similar to their physical counterparts, emotional painkillers bring their own set of side effects. One of the most notable side effects is the numbing of our emotions. Through constant suppression of our pain, we gradually lose touch with the layers of our authentic feelings. We inadvertently construct a shield that blunts our sensitivity, making it increasingly challenging to differentiate between what's genuine and what's masked. The peril lies in this state of numbness. Picture years of burying our pain, only to discover that it never truly vanishes. It lingers beneath the surface, silently wreaking havoc on our mental, emotional and spiritual equilibrium. We find ourselves disconnected from our genuine selves, traversing life through a haze of confusion and disillusionment. Relying on emotional painkillers merely feeds into the cycle of imbalance and emotional fragility. It's akin to placing a band-aid on a wound that requires stitches. While it may offer some relief, it fails to address the root problem. With time, the wound festers, causing more harm than healing.

Emotional painkillers have a peculiar addictive quality that often stems from the human tendency to seek an escape from the challenging realities of life. We all possess our vices – those outlets we turn to for relief or distraction. These seemingly harmless vices can become addictive because they provide a way to momentarily detach from the turmoil unfolding in our lives. In this context, emotional painkillers serve as the gateway to these vices, working dually. Initially, there's emotional denial, a mechanism by which we convince ourselves that the pain we're under-going, whether it's feelings of rejection, abandon-ment, or other emotional triggers, isn't truly real or isn't our responsibility to address.

Yet, even as we try to suppress these feelings, our subconscious remains aware of the authentic truth behind these emotional triggers. This conflict within us propels us toward physical vices. This can manifest as seeking solace in food, alcohol, drugs, sex, technology. Essentially, anything that can divert our attention from the distressing emotions we're grappling with.

Regrettably, the aftermath of avoiding the reality of this pain is the accumulation of emotional stress and other health-related prob-lems. This process creates an unnecessary harmful cycle. As long as we continue evading the honest confrontation of our pain, it accumu-lates, leading to amplified stress and other complications. It's indeed a vicious cycle and as long as we persistently refuse to acknowledge the existence of our pain bravely, we're destined to be caught in the web of deep-seated agony or profound denial. The key lies in breaking this cycle by daring to face and process our emotions head-on, a journey that ultimately brings us closer to healing and growth.

Embarking on our *Say Yes* journey requires a deep dive into understanding our emotional trig-gers and the unconscious tendency to suppress them with emotional painkillers. It's like shining a light on the shadowy corners we've avoided for so long. Emotional triggers are those sensitive spots within us, often tied to past experiences, that can set off a cascade of emotions. They're like old wounds that haven't completely healed. In our attempt to avoid the discomfort they bring, we often resort to using emotional painkillers, which are mechanisms that temporarily mask the pain. It's a coping strategy we might not even be consciously aware of. I distinctly recall a moment on my journey when I caught myself reaching for that emotional painkiller. Instead of swallowing it down, though, I accidentally ingested a different kind of truth – the kind that gives you that undeniable lump in your throat. It was a moment of raw honesty with myself. That lump was the signal that I could no longer deny the reality of my emotions and the triggers causing them. This experience became a turning point, a wake-up call to the fact that I had been relying on emotional painkillers for far too long. This journey encourages us to recognize and confront these patterns, even if it's uncomfortable at first.

As I've mentioned before and will keep reminding you, this is a process – a journey that unfolds at its own pace. Depending on where you stand in your journey, the information shared might either plant a seed of awareness or take root as a budding understanding deep within. Trust me, this transformation can be both painful and unexpectedly joyful, but it requires effort and commitment. Healing and transformation are seldom without their challenges. Just like labor is a painful process for both the mother and the baby, our transformation can be uncomfortable. We might not remember the details of our entry into this world, but it doesn't mean the process was painless.

Similarly, I used to resist change fiercely. However, the weight of continued emotional pain led me to a point where I had to seek a different path. Now, I'm here, fully engaged in doing the work to heal and grow. I've realized that embracing this journey means showing up for myself, for life and, by extension, for others and humanity. We're all in the same boat of pain, often pointing fingers at others, but at some juncture, we must take ownership of our parts, acknowledging our role in the narrative. Only through this ownership can we become the change we wish to witness in the world around us.

Learned Emotional Behavior

Indeed, the paths through which we unconsciously take emotional painkillers can be divided into two distinct levels: learned emotional behavior and the mask protector. Everything that shapes us and defines our actions directly results from the environment we grow up in. How we experience and outwardly display our emotions is a learned response developed for survival. As the primary figures in our early lives, our parents greatly influence this. It's often stated that we learn best through observation, not just through listening. This implies that our focus is more on actions than words. Actions, after all, have a more profound impact than verbal communication.

I was raised in a religious cult where families were separated into distinct quarters - women and children on one side, men and boys on the other.

This arrangement meant that I spent most of my time under the care of another member who oversaw a group of about ten children. For nearly a decade, my parents were a rare sight, only coming into view once or twice a week or as much as the cult allowed. It might sound unusual, but I adapted and normalized this unique circumstance.

In the cult, emotional expressions like love and compassion took a backseat to discipline and devotion. The focus was on serving a higher purpose and following the cult's doctrines. Then came the moment of leaving that secluded world and reentering society with my family. This shift was like stepping into a realm of strangers, even though they were my blood. Family separation and someone else's influence overtook those vital years of understanding and bonding. When I reflect on my parents' relationship, I remember very few instances of physical affection or public displays of affection (PDA). My mom, who did many of the caretaking responsibilities, poured her emotions and time into looking after my father and us children. She was a selfless care-taker, often placing herself last. This self-sacrifice, witnessed over the years, could unconsciously shape one's survival strategy. It was apparent that her happiness and fulfillment took a backseat, which is why I was determined to live differently. However, as life would have it, and as the saying goes: "The road to hell was paved with good intentions." Meaning our intentions don't always translate seamlessly into reality. The complexities of life often challenge our well-intended plans. It's a thought that often crosses my mind: could observe my mother consistently placing herself last be where I unknowingly learned not to prioritize myself? Reflecting on this makes me question whether I unknowingly absorbed the habit of denying my own needs. When I became a parent, I was unsure if I managed to break away from these learned behaviors. My marriage ended in divorce and I lost full custody of my children, a stark contrast from my parents' experience.

The concept of learned emotional behavior is intriguing. It's like a secret language we inherit, teaching us how to manage and conceal our feelings. Like my parents, I found it hard to express love and emotions to my children openly. While they may have witnessed love through discipline and punishment, it's only half of what's needed. My parents had their share of disagreements, adding a layer of irony to my story. In my last and longest relationship, I was determined to rise above the constant complaints and disappointment that my parents seemed to embody. I was determined not to repeat that cycle, but looking back, I see now how my partner would point out moments when I acted just like my mom. I couldn't see it clearly back then, but now, it's become evident post-separation. Despite my intentions, I somehow mirrored my mother's emotional behavior.

Recognizing these patterns, these echoes of past generations is crucial. It begs the question: Who is responsible for breaking the cycle of learned emotional behavior? It's a question that places the power of change squarely in our hands. It's a journey of understanding, unlearning and forging a new way of relating to our emotions, ourselves and those around us. It's important to grasp that the emotional behavior we've absorbed is a result of learning, not a reflection of our authentic selves. To truly understand this, we must open ourselves up and allocate time for introspection, diving into the underlying reasons for our learned emotional responses. While I can't fully speak for my parents' motivations, I can certainly delve into my own. It's clear to me that fear played a significant role in shaping my emotional patterns. This fear encompassed the dread of losing, the anxiety of making mistakes and the worry of being judged for what I now recognize as normal human missteps. It's a truth of life that we learn through trial and error, through moments of stumbling and getting back up again. The journey to understanding ourselves requires us to unravel the influences that shaped us.

By acknowledging that these emotional patterns are learned rather than inherent, we create space for growth and transformation. It's a journey of self-discovery, learning to be kinder to ourselves and granting ourselves the freedom to embrace our humanity with all its imperfections.

The Protector

Think about those superhero movies we've all watched: *The Mask, Superman, Black Panther, Spider-Man, Wonder Woman* and more. You know, the characters who seem to gain superpowers when they wear their special outfits. It's like clothes are the key to unlocking their inner strength, but do these heroes need their masks and capes to be powerful?

In my view, those masks and capes are more than just accessories. They're symbols of self-belief and empowerment. Sure, the heroes had the power within them all along, but the mask and cape acted as a boost button for their confidence. They believed they needed that extra layer of protection to embrace their strength fully. What if that external source of power suddenly disappears? What happens when the mask and cape aren't enough? Where do these heroes turn to find their strength, then? It's a question we can relate to in our own lives. We might not wear actual masks and capes, but we wear metaphorical ones. We put on different faces for different situations while convincing ourselves that we're confident and in control. Yet, deep down, we know the truth. We're on a journey where we've been wearing masks and superhero capes, but secretly struggling to maintain that image.

And when we finally remove the mask and expose our vulnerabilities and flaws, who are we? Where do we find that same strength we had when we were hiding behind our masks and capes? This journey is about discovering that the strength was never just in the mask or cape. It was always within us. It's about finding the courage to be ourselves unapologetically, unfiltered and unmasked. When the external crutches are gone, we find the real wellspring of strength waiting patiently for us to tap into it. And that discovery is where the true hero's journey begins.

We've all crafted our masks, just like those superheroes donning masks and capes to become invincible. These symbols of power make them seem unbeatable, but the truth is, when those masks come off, they're just as vulnerable as anyone else. Our masks serve a similar purpose: they shield us from pain, discomfort and vulnerability. They're our armor against the world's blows, but what happens when we realize that relying solely on that mask puts us in a risky spot? Maybe it's time to focus on strengthening our authentic selves so we can confidently face the world without needing a protective facade. So, how did we end up crafting these masks and capes? Life happened, as it tends to do. Life isn't always a smooth ride; it throws curveballs that we might not like. Maybe we faced some emotional and physical challenges. In those moments, we instinctively put on our masks, fighting for survival while pretending everything's fine. And while things might be okay, we've somehow convinced ourselves that not getting what we want is a catastrophe. So, we throw on our metaphorical tantrum-fueled masks, pretending to be someone we're not, all hoping to manipulate our way to fulfill our desires.

Let's be real; this act can only last so long. Manipulation isn't a sustainable strategy. It might bring short-term gains, but it is not the foundation for a meaningful life. The real strength lies in embracing who we are, with all our imperfections and vulnerabilities. It's about realizing that life's challenges aren't necessarily a punishment; they're opportunities for growth and resilience. As we shed our masks and capes, we enter our true power, navigating the world with authenticity and courage. The journey of unmasking ourselves is an intriguing and somewhat unsettling experience. It's as if we're peeling away a fixed, false identity that we've presented to the world and ourselves. This process can feel strange, almost like we're revealing ourselves to a stranger despite being intimately acquainted with this hidden side. A certain discomfort accompanies this unveiling, like shedding a protective layer that's been a part of us for so long. And even if we try to put that mask back on, it's never the same. It's like an adhesive that loses its stickiness once removed: it just won't adhere as tightly as before.

This is a critical realization and it's why even superheroes eventually meet their end. Like them, our masks and capes must also meet their demise if we aspire to lead genuine, fulfilling lives. They've served their purpose, offering protection and strength when needed, but also limiting our authenticity and growth. So, we must let them go, allowing our true selves to emerge. Only when we shed these layers can we truly embrace life in its unfiltered, authentic form. It's remarkably easy to point fingers at others, accusing them of being phony and wearing masks and capes, but we often forget that we're also speaking about ourselves. Passing judgment on someone as if we're flawless and have never projected a false image is a form of self-deception. Accusing others is, in essence, accusing ourselves of the same thing.

There's no need to judge ourselves or others harshly for leading lives that sometimes feel fraudulent. It's a behavior we've all learned, a survival mechanism. Our authentic selves often didn't stand a chance, especially when we were children.

We were too frightened and small to confront injustice head-on, so we adopted pretenses and played a part to survive. The irony lies in the fact that we've all been there and it's an aspect of our collective human experience.

CHAPTER TWO

The River Of De Nile

Denial is precisely what its name suggests: a state of denial. At some point or another, we all have denied that we were in denial, which illustrates how powerful denial can be. It can trick you into thinking that you're perfectly fine when, actually, you're in deep denial. Denial and emotional painkillers are closely related; they make it unnecessarily difficult for us to progress toward transformation. However, the truth is that it's challenging to confront our shortcomings. Denial provides us with an escape into a fantasy world, even if that fantasy doesn't align with the harsh reality of our lives. My father used to say, "There you go, swimming in the river of De-Nile" and I didn't fully grasp the meaning until later in adulthood, after years of unnecessary hardship.

Denial is our security blanket, shielding our

emotions and belief systems like nothing else. Many people aren't even aware of the level or depth of denial they're in because the pain is too unbearable to confront. Instead, they prefer to remain distracted, avoiding the painful truth concealed beneath their denial. Denial has often cast a spell upon us, causing us to wander through life, ignoring all the signs pointing toward healing. We become too afraid to let go of our security blanket, acknowledge those signs for what they truly are and step out of our comfort zones, even when we're deeply unfulfilled. As a result, denial stretches our journey toward transformation, making it unnecessarily long.

Unconsciously, we resist the natural flow of life, clinging stubbornly to what we desire and believe, even when life repeatedly confronts us with obstacles, unhappiness and unfulfillment. Our fixed, masked identity convinces us that it's our true self.

So, when our loved ones or even strangers point out an alternative path or life sends us countless signs, we often ignore them because we've convinced ourselves that the masked persona represents our authentic self.

Denial often plays a cruel trick on us. It convinces us that if we say our feelings aren't hurt or that we "don't care," it must be the truth. I, too, used to frequently use the phrase "I don't care" to the point where I questioned whether I genuinely didn't care anymore. I said it so much that my body began to believe it and life seemed to provide me with ample opportunities to live in the realm of "I don't care." Many of us proudly utter these words as if not caring is a sign of strength, as if we are unaffected by life's challenges, but the reality is that if we truly didn't care, we wouldn't need to say it repeatedly. It would be evident in our actions. Yet, often, our actions don't align with the behavior of someone who genuinely doesn't care. Refusing to acknowledge our feelings, to admit that we care, can be detrimental. It leaves no room for healing or clarity because we continue to deny the existence of our genuine feelings. While there may indeed be times when we genuinely don't care, we do care most of the time and that's perfectly okay. If we can admit to our feelings of caring, we've already won half the battle against denial.

Denial can often serve as a form of self-handicap rooted in fear. This fear runs so deep and is so paralyzing that we hold onto our denial even as it slowly erodes us from within. We're terrified of exposure, not just to others, but also to ourselves. We fear being at the center of shame, ridicule and embarrassment. Think back to those childhood days when innocence still held our hearts. Picture this: You're hanging out with your friends, and suddenly, they decide to snatch some candy from the corner store, but you, being the "good child," recognize the potential trouble and fear of getting caught. So, you decline their offer. Not understanding the weight of your decision, your friends begin to tease you mercilessly, calling you a "scaredy-cat." This scenario can take many forms, but let's imagine you held your ground and refused to steal. As you walk home, their taunts continue, labeling you as the "scaredy-cat." The next day, on the playground, the name-calling persists. You find yourself at a crossroads. Do you continue enduring the ridicule, being shamed by your only friends in the neighborhood? Or do you give in and steal with them next time, hoping to end the ridicule and gain acceptance? This is the precarious dance we often find ourselves in, trapped between our fear of judgment and our desire for connection. Denial becomes our crutch, shielding us from the vulnerability of being true to ourselves. It's a coping mechanism we adopt to fit into a world that may not fully understand or appreciate our choices.

The moment of decision has arrived. The time has come for you to join your friends in their act of stealing. As you take that step towards conformity, a curious transformation begins within you. You find yourself attempting to convince your mind that you stole because you genuinely wanted to, not because you dreaded being labeled a "scaredy-cat." And thus, denial makes its entrance, starting its subtle dance with your consciousness. This is how denial takes root. It takes hold early on in our lives as we strive to convince ourselves that we are just like everyone else, fitting the mold of what is "normal." It is a harsh reality that we all face, for no matter which path the child in our story would have chosen, it ultimately leads to conformity. Such is the nature of life's intricate dance. In doing so, we gradually convince ourselves that the person we conform to is our true self, but we were hidden beneath the layers of illusion. Deep within the recesses of our being lies our true self, buried beneath the sands of the playground, lost amidst the tides of conformity. It is time for a grand treasure hunt, a quest to uncover the authentic version of yourself. In its divine design, life created each of us perfectly as we are. Our insecurities and doubts led us to believe we were not enough, that we needed to conform to belong and quell the pangs of loneliness.

Denial is nothing but a clever disguise, just like emotional painkillers are a form of denial in disguise. Can you spot the pattern here?

We create myriad excuses, fabricating reasons why we should remain as we are and why we don't need to embark on the transformative journey towards our authentic selves. These excuses become our shield, allowing us to continue living under the facade of a false identity.

I am no stranger to excuses. I was once the reigning queen of justifications, always ready with an explanation for every aspect of my being. I always had my "why" ready: why I am this way? Why I like certain things? Why I don't like this, that, or others? We've become so deeply entrenched in this charade that we have convinced ourselves to live authentically. We've sold this false image of ourselves to others and now we are bound to uphold it at any cost, even if it means sacrificing our well-being.

However, It doesn't have to be this way. We can shed the layers of pretense and reclaim our true selves. We can break free from the chains of conformity and enter our authenticity's radiant light. The fear of judgment and the discomfort of change may try to pull us back into the safety of our false identity, but we must summon our courage, for the rewards of living as our genuine selves far outweigh the temporary comfort of conformity. So, let us strip away the excuses, exposing them for what they truly are.

Denial may provide temporary relief, a slight safety moment, but it's a false refuge. It keeps us stagnant, bound by the expectations of others rather than embracing our authenticity. Denying our feelings and refusing to acknowledge their existence can be dangerous territory. The first step towards liberation from denial is admitting our caring nature.

By embracing our feelings and acknowledging that we care, we create space for healing, growth and a deeper understanding of ourselves. Let's release the façade of indifference and allow ourselves to acknowledge the truth. Let's honor our caring hearts and be open to the emotions that shape our experiences. In doing so, we embark on a transformative journey of self-discovery, where denial loses its grip and the authentic power of our feelings takes center stage. Embrace the beauty of caring, for it is through caring that we connect with ourselves and the world around us profoundly and meaningfully.

The Blame Game

Now that we have explored how we conform to societal norms in order to find acceptance, love and survival in a world that rejected our innocent selves, let's take a closer look at our current state as adults. We find ourselves experiencing a range of emotions: unhappiness, dissatisfaction, misery, bitterness, anger, jealousy and selfishness, as well as moments of happiness, love, spontaneity, adventure, success and wealth.

This rollercoaster cycle seems never-ending. We strive to eliminate the negative aspects of ourselves, those parts we adopted to survive, hoping to create a better life. However, we find ourselves dissatisfied with the results we see. Despite our denial telling us that we are doing everything right, we constantly encounter setbacks and things seem to go wrong sometimes all the way wrong.

In our frustration, we often resort to blaming others. We question why, as "the good person" who strives to treat others well, we are the ones experiencing suffering, rejection, heartbreak, anger and jealousy, which leaves us to believe that someone or something external is interfering with the positive outcomes we expect and deserve. It becomes convenient to shift responsibility away from ourselves and onto others. But are we truly being honest with ourselves? Are we truly embodying the values and actions we claim to uphold? Our experiences and outcomes are shaped not only by external factors, but also by our choices, attitudes and behaviors. Blaming others absolves us of personal accountability and shields us from facing the uncomfortable truth that we may have contributed to our unhappiness and unfulfillment. By placing the blame externally, we avoid taking an honest look within ourselves and examining our actions and their consequences. It's natural to question whether life is playing a cruel game with us or if we've misunderstood the "do unto others as you would have them do unto you" quote. What if the essence of the quote is that our actions towards others reflect how we treat ourselves or have been treated? It's worth considering, as it prompts us to pause and examine our thoughts and behaviors. Denial thrives on our need to assign blame for our misfortunes, unhappiness, anger and resentment.

Denial insists that we must find someone to

hold responsible. In turn, we rely on others to bring us joy and happiness, leaving us powerless and susceptible to becoming victims of our circumstances. It may not be easy to accept, but it's the truth. I've been there myself, blaming my parents for not being the ideal version of themselves and for not loving me in the way I desired. After all, I reasoned, I'm the child and they're the adults who should know better and naturally possess the ability to love. But the reality is they, like us, conformed imperfect beings. As humans, we often impose unrealistic expectations on others, including ourselves. However, we tend to hold others to higher standards and expectations than ourselves. This perpetuates a vicious cycle and blame, along with denial and emotional painkillers, swim in the same pool of our lives. This cycle of blame and denial creates drama and turmoil, further complicating our journey. Blaming others allows us to assume the role of a helpless victim, avoiding any sense of personal accountability or the need for change on our part. We convince ourselves that it's other people who must change in order for our circumstances or outcomes to improve. However, reflecting on the saying, "Be the change you want to see in the world," it becomes clear that expecting change while solely blaming others is illogical. It's almost like a form of insanity. I've been caught in the cycle of blaming others for my troubles. My list of grievances was extensive, but I grew weary of repeating the same patterns.

The question arises: why do we tend to blame others for the difficulties and pain we encounter? Could it be simpler to point fingers outward rather than turn the spotlight on ourselves? Are we so detached from our reality that we fail to see our contribution to the outcomes in our lives? Perhaps when we accept responsibility for the results, we're compelled to acknowledge our role in creating them. The blame game doesn't benefit anyone, not even the accused. Life has repeatedly shown us that assigning blame to others doesn't resolve our problems or the world's problems. We must actively engage in self-awareness and modify our behavior to bring about change. The pain and disappointment we experience are often the consequences of our actions. This may be a bitter truth, but it remains the truth. Nothing will change unless we open our minds to shift our perspectives, potentially leading us to a new way of living. In the book "The Four Agreements" by Don Miguel Ruiz, he emphasizes the importance of not taking things personally. When we take things personally, we become victims of someone else's actions and their right to choose. If we begin to practice not taking things personally, we can start to dismantle the idea of an external enemy on which we place all our troubles. Recognizing that we are all products of society and the values it instilled in us, we realize that taking things personally aligns with the blame game. We must summon the strength and courage to confront our flaws and self-defecation, liberating ourselves from the grip of others and their right to behave as we please. This shift allows us to stop blaming them for how we feel and react to their actions against us.

When we take a step back and truly examine our experiences, it becomes evident that changing the players involved doesn't necessarily yield different outcomes. It's the common denominator that requires observation and transformation. Perhaps we are the common denominator and the ones to hold accountable. It's empowering to realize that change begins within ourselves. Blaming others only perpetuates the cycle of frustration and disappointment. Instead, we must reflect on our thoughts, actions and choices—the factors we can control. It's in our hands to initiate the change we desire. By acknowledging our role in the outcomes we experience, we can break free from the pattern of blame and start making meaningful changes in our lives. This shift in mindset and taking responsibility for our growth and transformation is a liberating process. However, by releasing the need to blame others and focusing on personal development, we open ourselves up to new possibilities and a greater sense of fulfillment. So, let's pause and reconsider our tendency to blame. Instead of dwelling on external factors, let's direct our energy towards self-exploration and personal growth. By doing so, we become active participants in our own lives, capable of creating and shaping the outcomes we desire.

The Busy Bee

Blaming others and external circumstances for our unhappiness sets in motion a strange paradox. As we point fingers outward, we paradoxically come to believe that these external elements are responsible for our joy and overall well-being. This belief makes us cautious and hesitant to engage with new people or situations. We carry the heavy baggage of past disappointments and unmet expectations, holding others or circumstances accountable. This emotional baggage often makes us feel like the sunshine has been drained from our lives. To shield ourselves from this perceived negativity, we unconsciously turn to busyness. We convince ourselves that staying busy will protect us from reliving similar pain and unwanted experiences. Our schedules become packed and constantly filled with tasks, commitments and distractions. It's a way to escape the discomfort and vulnerability that might accompany opening ourselves up to new connections, unexpected outcomes, or moments of stillness.

Our relentless pursuit of busyness often closes our eyes to the core issue. This issue stems from our fear of encountering pain and disappointment, causing us to attribute our happiness solely to external factors. By continually immersing ourselves in busyness, we hope to exert control over our lives, shielding ourselves from the perceived negativity that external factors might bring. Isn't it intriguing how we find comfort in the concept of busyness? In our society, busyness is frequently linked to productivity and success. It's deeply woven into the fabric of the American dream. We are determined to steer clear of any labels that suggest laziness or unproductivity, yearning instead for lives that earn approval from our families and society.

We crave recognition as individuals who are excelling in their pursuits. In our relentless pursuit of this elusive ideal life, we adamantly refuse to allow mishaps, setbacks, heartbreak, or even our denial to impede our progress. We continue to forge ahead, no matter the obstacles, even if it means limping on an injured leg. We've grown so accustomed to pain that we've convinced ourselves that as long as we keep moving, we're on the right path to happiness and success. We've transformed into perpetual travelers, constantly hopping from one destination to the next, always searching for the next milestone.

This has become our way of life, our very identity. We've warmly embraced busyness as a shield against our unresolved emotions. By filling every moment with tasks and responsibilities, we deftly dodge any deep introspection into our innermost thoughts and feelings. There's a fear that if we pause for too long, we might stumble upon a glitch in the elaborate fantasy we've meticulously crafted. The habit of staying busy can often become our sanctuary, offering a comforting sense of security by keeping our minds and hearts perpetually engaged. It's as if there's never enough time to be still, turn inward and face our emotions. This is where the allure of emotional painkillers and denial gains its power, as they shield us from the depths of our emotional world.

But now, it's paramount that we open ourselves to vulnerability and embark on a journey into the uncharted territory of our emotional realm. It's not that productivity itself is inherently unhealthy; rather, it's about examining the how and why behind our productivity. We might realize that we're investing an excessive amount of time and energy fixating on the actions of others instead of directing our focus toward the change we have the power to effect in our lives. Perhaps we find ourselves spending hours watching television, engaging in endless phone conversations with friends, or indulging in excessive social activities—all under the guise of living life and having fun. While it's undoubtedly important to relish life and find enjoyment, we must also reserve time for self-reflection and healing.

Denial often whispers to us, convincing us that we bear no responsibility, just as emotional painkillers deceive us into believing we don't feel. This perpetuates the vicious cycle in which excessive busyness entangles us in our drama, leading us to believe that it's others who must change for our external world to transform. However, the wisdom of "as within, so without" reminds us that our inner state reflects our outer world. If our external reality is dominated by busyness, chaos and unhealthy patterns, it's essential to pause and honestly assess what's truly transpiring within. Taking a step back and honestly evaluating our situation grants us the opportunity to uncover the underlying patterns and behaviors contributing to our present circumstances. It's a chance to confront our role in shaping our reality and explore how we can initiate changes from within. As children, our lives were enriched with the joy of play. We could immerse ourselves in imaginative adventures involving our cherished toys, playground escapades, skating, jump rope, or sandbox creations. These activities could captivate us for hours, rendering us oblivious to the growling hunger and nagging thirst that would occasionally demand our attention. In this analogy, hunger and thirst symbolize our emotions and authentic selves, silently craving recognition and fulfillment. Yet, amidst the enchanting whirlwind of our play-filled world, we often failed to grasp the importance of pausing. We overlooked the value of taking a moment to catch our breath, nourish our bodies and quench our thirst. Thankfully, with their wisdom and perspective, adults understood the vital need for sustenance in our lives. They intervened in our playtime, introducing moments of respite where we could eat, reflect and connect with our loved ones. It's perfectly natural to be spellbound by the allure of the sandbox. However, achieving a healthy balance is essential. We must learn to be more present in reality, recognizing the significance of nurturing our physical, emotional and spiritual well-being. Just as our bodies require sustenance to thrive, our emotions and authentic selves deserve attention. Through this harmonious integration of play and self-care, we can navigate life with a sense of equilibrium and fulfillment. It can be quite challenging when we notice patterns repeating from generation to generation. We often look at our parents and grandparents and wonder if they ever truly experienced joy and happiness. While some undoubtedly did, many might not have had the same experience, which is why these cycles persist. We are, by nature, creatures of learned behavior. We commonly adopt certain behaviors and attitudes based on what we've observed from our families. We may have seen our predecessors stay busy, tirelessly pursuing a better life for us. However, the outcomes are never guaranteed to deliver the improved life we hoped for.

In response, we may easily blame them for the ups and downs we encounter in our pursuit of busyness. This occurs because we haven't fully understood and embraced our true selves. Instead, we often strive to meet the expectations of others, merely following the established paths of our families. It's almost as if survival becomes our primary goal and settling for less becomes the accepted norm. We may even resort to staying busy to avoid confronting our truths and the need for change.

You deserve more than mere survival in the pursuit of a busy life. You deserve fulfillment, self-love and genuine joy. It's time to break free from this generational cycle and challenge the status quo. Embrace your authentic self and forge a new path. Take a pause to contemplate what truly brings you happiness and purpose. Question the beliefs and patterns that have been handed down to you. Dare to stand out and disrupt this cycle. You don't have to settle for a life consumed by busyness and avoidance. It's time to step into your power and construct a life that harmonizes with your genuine desires and values. Remember the lessons imparted by those wise adults who emphasize the importance of pausing, recharging and nurturing connections.

By balancing our playful moments with introspection, self-care and meaningful interactions, we thrive in our reality and cultivate a deeply satisfying existence. It's in finding this healthy equilibrium that we can genuinely relish the joy of play while respecting our innate emotional needs and savoring the richness of our human connections.

CHAPTER THREE

Relationship Stimulations

It's indeed intriguing how relationships and happiness often dominate conversations about success. The concept of a perfect couple and relationship goals has become a prominent trend and it seems everyone is pursuing this ideal. It appears that somewhere along the way, we've adopted the belief that our entire identity and true fulfillment are dependent on our relationships. We've come to believe that finding that special someone is the only path to genuine success and happiness. However, reality often doesn't align with this belief. When we enter into relationships, the outcomes often fall short of our expectations, far from the fairy-tale endings we envision.

So, how did we evolve into a society seemingly obsessed with having a significant other, even if that person doesn't entirely meet our specific desires? Why do we often find ourselves settling in relationships, even when it might not be in our best interest?

Perhaps pursuing a relationship with ourselves isn't as popular because we've become addicted to the stimulation of external relationships. We seek validation of our self-worth through these relationships, seeking confirmation and fulfillment from others rather than cultivating it from within. This societal shift has made it crucial for us to explore the concepts of self-love, self-fulfillment and self-relationship to achieve a more balanced and genuine sense of happiness and success.

Relationships indeed hold a special place in our lives and they can bring immense joy, companionship and fulfillment. It's entirely natural to desire deep connections and love. However, it's essential to recognize that being in a relationship isn't the sole determinant of our worth or happiness.

In today's society, there's often an unspoken expectation that if you're successful, attractive, or have your life together, you should also have a partner. It's almost like having a significant other becomes a checkbox on the list of societal expectations. This expectation can sometimes lead to loneliness or self-doubt when someone isn't in a relationship, even if they're thriving in other aspects of their life. We must challenge this societal norm and remember that our relationship status doesn't define our worth. Being content with yourself, building a meaningful relationship and nurturing self-love are equally important journeys in life. These internal connections can bring about a sense of fulfillment and completeness that complements, rather than depends on, external relationships.

There's a common belief that a woman who possesses both beauty and financial success and a partner by her side has achieved some pinnacle in life. It's not just about appearances or wealth; it's the idea that having a partner validates your worth and value. This societal conditioning can be frustrating and even disheartening. The comparisons people make to reality shows or others who seemingly have found love can be particularly distressing. It's natural to wonder why you may still be searching for a romantic partner despite feeling like you're doing everything right and having attractive qualities. It's important to remember that each person's journey in life is unique. Comparing ourselves to others, especially in romantic relationships, can be detrimental to our self-esteem and well-being. Finding love and building a meaningful relationship can be influenced by various factors, including timing, circumstances and personal growth. Focusing on self-love, personal growth and building a strong relationship with oneself can often lead to healthier and more fulfilling connections with others when the time is right.

Growing up in a cult, my life was handed a script with a rigid narrative. According to this script, my purpose revolved around serving both

God and Man. I was taught to nurture my spirit for the satisfaction of God and to take care of my physical body to meet the needs of men and my future family. Yet, it seemed to omit one crucial aspect – nurturing myself and my desires and aspirations. The cult's definition of a "good" woman included traits like being well-behaved, soft-spoken and subservient, often walking several steps behind a man. These expectations were not only unrealistic, but sometimes even comical. This conditioning permeated every facet of my life, leaving little room for self-discovery or personal growth.

As a child, a fire burned within me, yearning to rebel against these expectations. Conforming to the norms within the cult felt like attempting to fit a square peg into a round hole. I was in a constant internal struggle, torn between my longing to be my authentic self and the fear of being ostracized for not adhering to the mold of a well-behaved girl. This deep-seated indoctrination makes me wonder: is this the root of our addiction to relationship stimulation? None of us wants to be cast aside or left alone. From a young age, we're conditioned to believe that our purpose is to conform, to be the "good person" who adheres to societal norms in the hope of attracting the perfect mate. Once we find that ideal partner, we often unconsciously become reliant on their presence in our lives. We start to believe that they hold the key to our overall well-being. This belief extends to our family and friends as well. Those close to us, we begin to think, are the primary source of our highs and lows, the judges of our good and bad times. While we may hope for more good than bad, even during challenging times, we convince ourselves to stay in the relationship or settle for less. Society has ingrained in us that having a significant other is superior to being alone. We've internalized the notion that being desired somehow validates our worth and value. It's as if we're in a perpetual quest to be the "good person" who attracts and retains a partner by doing everything in our power to make them happy.

In today's fast-paced and ever-changing world, it does seem like relationships are more fragile than ever. The high separation and divorce rates are indeed concerning and it's essential to explore why this is happening. One significant factor in the fragility of relationships is the lack of self-awareness and self-trust. We often become so preoccupied with meeting societal expectations and conforming to external standards that we neglect to listen to our inner voices and desires. The foundation of any healthy and lasting relationship, whether with a partner, family member, or friend, starts with a strong and healthy relationship with oneself. Self-awareness, self-trust and self-love are crucial elements in building and maintaining meaningful connections. When we are in tune with our needs, values and boundaries, we can communicate more effectively and authentically with others. Ultimately, we have the power to shape our relationships by first shaping our relationship with ourselves. It involves introspection, self-reflection and a willingness to grow and evolve as individuals. When both partners in a relationship have a solid foundation of self-awareness and self-trust, they can work together to create a strong, resilient and fulfilling connection. Self-love and self-acceptance play a crucial role in our ability to have healthy and fulfilling relationships. If we're not clear about our own identity and what truly matters to us, it can be challenging to communicate our needs and expectations effectively to others.

When we have a strong foundation of self-love, we become less dependent on external validation or the fulfillment of our needs by others. We understand that it's our responsibility to fill our cups emotionally and mentally.

This shift towards self-responsibility can lead to healthier dynamics in relationships because we're not burdening others with the sole task of meeting our emotional needs. Confidence and self-belief are attractive qualities because they often reflect a secure person in themselves and their identity. When we accept ourselves without judgment and embrace our uniqueness, we radiate that confidence, making us more appealing to others. In essence, building a strong relationship with ourselves is empowering and paves the way for more authentic and fulfilling connections with others. It allows us to enter relationships as whole individuals, ready to share our lives rather than seeking someone to complete us. An important point to consider is the concept of unconditional love and the unrealistic expectations that can sometimes permeate relationships. Many individuals enter relationships with certain expectations and conditions that they believe must be met for the relationship to be deemed successful or worthy.

This can create a dynamic where both partners constantly try to fulfill these expectations, leading to stress, disappointment and a sense of being unfulfilled. On the other hand, unconditional love is about loving someone for who they truly are, flaws and all, without expecting them to change to meet your ideals or conditions while establishing healthy boundaries for yourself. It's about accepting each other with all your imperfections and differences. This form of love often leads to more authentic and lasting connections. While relationships can bring joy and companionship to our lives, they shouldn't be the sole source of our happiness or the determinant of our success. Individuals need to find fulfillment within themselves first, to have a sense of self-worth and purpose that isn't dependent on external factors like a romantic relationship.

A healthy and successful relationship should complement your life rather than define it entirely. It should be built on mutual respect, understanding and acceptance. It's not about suppressing yourself to fit someone else's expectations, but finding someone who loves and appreciates you for your authentic self. The fear of being alone is a common and deeply ingrained one. Many people fear solitude because it often forces them to confront themselves, their thoughts and their emotions more directly. However, being comfortable with yourself and having a positive relationship is essential before seeking it from others. When we love and respect ourselves, we set the standard for how we want to be treated by others and we're less likely to settle for unhealthy or unfulfilling relationships. Being alone doesn't mean being lonely or unloved. It can be a time of self-discovery, personal growth and inner reflection. Embracing solitude allows you to understand who you truly are, what you value and what brings you joy. It's an opportunity to build a strong sense of self-worth that isn't dependent on external validation.

By shifting the focus from seeking validation through relationships to embracing self-love and self-discovery, we can redefine what relationships mean and create connections based on authenticity and mutual respect. It's an ongoing journey that offers the chance to craft meaningful relationships that align with our true selves while finding contentment within ourselves, regardless of our relationship status.

Resentment: Giving vs Receiving

When we fixate on comparing our lives to others, we unknowingly surrender the beauty and blessings surrounding us daily. It's easy to talk about the importance of gratitude, but much harder to walk the path of true appreciation. Life, as it does, has its way of unfolding. And just like life, comparison has a job to do—it thrives on showing us how we measure up against others. It's become so ingrained in our daily routines that we unconsciously compare our outer worlds, assuming that a happy facade reflects the true depth of our inner emotions, but this misguided belief often leads us down a treacherous path of jealousy and resentment.

Resentment, I call it the silent killer. It creeps in unnoticed, its roots sinking deep within us until we are engulfed in its toxic grip, and all of this, is a direct result of our ceaseless comparisons. It robs us of the joy that could be ours and erodes the very foundation of gratitude. In our quest to navigate the complexities of comparison, we naturally focus on the surface level: observing what others possess or achieve in contrast to what we may lack. But what if there's another dimension to comparison? What if we investigate the subconscious tendency to compare what we give versus what we receive? At first glance, comparing what we give and receive might seem straightforward. We assess the balance between our efforts and the rewards we receive. However, as we peel back the layers, we discover that this process can be more intricate and multifaceted than meets the eye. Sometimes, we find ourselves giving abundantly, pouring our time, energy and resources into relationships, work and various endeavors. Yet, looking at what we receive in return may not always align with our expectations or the magnitude of our contributions. This disparity can lead to frustration, disappointment, or even resentment.

During my 10-year relationship, there was a long period when I took pleasure in being of service to my partner. I happily cooked dinner, cared for our children, offered foot rubs, back massages, facials and enjoyed intimate moments together. I relished the role of the "good girl-girlfriend," unaware that deep down, I secretly kept score of what I was giving versus what I was receiving in return. Looking back on my past relationships, it was a tough pill to swallow when I realized that I had fallen into the trap of comparing my giving to what the relationship provided me. This unhealthy shift in perspective had a detrimental effect on our connection. As the comparison continued, it silently invited resentment into our relationship—an insidious killer of love and harmony. Resentment is a cunning adversary. It creeps in undetected, slowly poisoning the bond between two people. Little did I realize that my constant comparison was paving the way for the growth of resentment within me. I had unknowingly set the stage for disappointment and frustration by focusing on what I believed I lacked in the relationship. I've understood the destructive power of comparison and the importance of cultivating a different mindset. Rather than keeping score and analyzing the balance of give and take, I've learned that relationships thrive on a foundation of unconditional love, compassion and selfless-ness. It's natural for us to evaluate what we give versus what we receive in our relationships, and sometimes, we can't help but feel that our part-ners haven't given their fair share. While it may seem unfair to harbor such feelings, the truth is that they can indeed exist. Resentment manifests silently, disguised as comparisons we make between ourselves and others.

This silent resentment allows us to bury our

true feelings about our partners, family, friends and even life itself. We hold a belief that we deserve the best, yet we find ourselves holding our loved ones accountable for the perceived lack and shortcomings we experience. We may silently compare our efforts and contributions with theirs, tallying up the imbalances in our minds.

I had no idea how deeply entrenched I was in resentment. Initially, I believed it was solely directed towards my partner, but in reality, it extended to everyone around me. Comparison, although it can have a healthy side, also carries a darker side. The negativity we perceive has its positive counterpart, just as the positivity we experience can have unhealthy aspects. This is the complex nature of reality. Resentment operates so subtly that we fail to recognize its presence until it's too late. It quietly festers within us, unnoticed, until it eventually leads us to act out in anger, seek revenge, or inflict pain upon others. It can take time to acknowledge the underlying resentment because we have conditioned ourselves to believe that someone else is responsible for our emotional state. Consequently, we strive to make them feel the same pain, disappointment and comparison we experience, inadvertently masking the truth: our inner unfulfillment and unresolved wounds in need of healing.

It's important to acknowledge and address these feelings, for they have the power to poison the love and connection we share. Instead of silently stewing in resentment, let us find the courage to have open and honest conversations with our partners, family and friends. By expressing our concerns, fears and needs, we create an opportunity for understanding and growth. Furthermore, it's crucial to remember that we are responsible for our happiness and fulfillment. While it's natural to desire support and reciprocation from our loved ones, placing the sole burden of our satisfaction on their shoulders can lead to disappointment and frustration. We must take ownership of our well-being and find ways to meet our needs independently. Instead of dwelling on what we perceive as shortcomings, let us shift our focus to gratitude and appreciation. Recognize the efforts and love our partners, family and friends provide, even if they may not always align with our expectations. If we find ourselves in this state of resentment, constantly comparing our giving to what we receive, could it be possible that our partner is also experiencing similar feelings? Can we imagine their resentment towards us and others as they, too, engage in their comparisons from their unique perspective? This is how resentment seeps into our relationships. It lies hidden, camouflaged deep within us, causing us to become coldhearted and disconnected from others and ourselves. Once healthy in its pursuit of self-care, our selfishness has become toxic. Resentment breeds resentment, creating a vicious cycle that eventually leads to regret.

Behaviors rooted in resentment often leave us remorseful, realizing that unhealthy comparisons drove our words and actions. The importance of authentic giving, setting boundaries and breaking free from the destructive pattern of resentment are incredibly valuable. Authentic giving is about sharing from the heart without expecting anything in return.

It's about finding joy and fulfillment in the act of giving itself rather than seeking validation or appreciation from others. This approach not only leads to more genuine and fulfilling relationships, but also helps in avoiding feelings of resentment. Resentment often arises when we give with expectations and feel unappreciated or taken for granted. Setting boundaries is a healthy way to ensure that our giving aligns with our desires and values. It allows us to say no, when necessary, without feeling guilty and to protect our emotional well-being. Recognizing the insidious nature of resentment is one of the Pink Print toward healing. It requires us to confront our own unmet needs and unhealed wounds. Self-reflection and personal growth play a significant role in this process. When we focus on our growth and self-awareness, we can release the grip of resentment and create a more compassionate and understanding environment in our relationships. Cultivating empathy and understanding for ourselves and others is crucial in fostering healthy and meaningful connections. Acknowledging our emotional struggles and approaching our relationships with empathy creates space for open and honest communication. This, in turn, allows us to seek genuine connection rather than engage in competition or comparison.

Who's Entitled?

L et's look at an important aspect of human behavior and social dynamics: entitlement. Entitlement often arises from the roles and titles we hold in society, whether it's our job titles, social statuses, or other forms of recognition. These titles can indeed carry a sense of power and authority, but they also raise questions about how we should wield that power responsibly. Possessing a title or a certain status should ideally come with a sense of responsibility. With power, whether big or small, comes the duty to consider how our actions and decisions affect not just ourselves, but also others and the broader community. Entitlement can sometimes cloud this sense of responsibility, leading individuals to believe they can act without consequences or consideration for others. Titles and roles are not just about personal privilege; they come with a social contract.

When we hold certain positions or designations, expectations and ethical standards are associated with them. Society often expects us to conform to certain norms and behaviors associated with these titles. However, this conformity can sometimes lead to a lack of sensitivity to the emotions and experiences of others. Titles and roles should not serve as a license to disregard the well-being of others. Entitlement can close our eyes to these potential harms. It's essential to actively counter this sense of entitlement by fostering empathy and a genuine concern for the feelings and experiences of others. This is not a weakness, but a strength that leads to more compassionate and harmonious relationships and communities. Each title has its expectations and navigating them can be quite demanding. The energy required to embody these various personas and fulfill the responsibilities that come with them can be overwhelming. In the process of managing these titles, we might feel unappreciated or undervalued. This can lead to frustration and a sense of disconnection.

It's also worth noting that while these titles are important and contribute to our identity, they don't define our entire being. We are complex individuals with unique qualities beyond the roles we play. Recognizing and embracing our authentic selves beyond the titles can be a liberating and empowering journey. It allows us to bring our genuine selves to each role, fostering more meaningful connections and a deeper sense of fulfillment in our lives. It serves as a reminder to reevaluate the roles and energy we invest in them, seeking a harmonious balance that aligns with our true selves. The universal struggle many of us face in today's world is the process of juggling these roles. We become so entangled in external expectations that we forget to nurture our inner essence. This disconnection can lead to feelings of emptiness and a longing for something more. The role of a mother indeed carries profound weight and responsibility, often rooted in love and a desire for the well-being of one's children. A mother's dedication and the sacrifices they make for our survival and honor are a testament to the depth of their love and commitment. Their actions were driven by a sense of responsibility tied to their role as a mother and their desire to protect us from the potential consequences of the world.

This intense focus on fulfilling the expectations of a title can also have unintended consequences. It can sometimes create pressure and limitations within relationships. The desire to ensure a child's success and avoid any perceived embarrassment may lead to a complex mix of emotions and interactions. While the multidimensional nature of titles and roles within families can provide love, support and guidance, they can also bring unique challenges and complexities. It's essential to recognize and appreciate the efforts made by those in these roles while acknowledging the need for balance and open communication within these relationships.

In the realms of romantic relationships, titles and labels can shape our behavior and expectations within these connections. Regarding dating, engagement, or marriage, titles can indeed profoundly impact how we perceive and navigate the relationship. Assigning titles often creates a sense of exclusivity, commitment and responsibility. While these can be positive aspects of a relationship, they can also lead to potential pitfalls. The feeling of entitlement, where one assumes certain rights or privileges within the relationship, can create tension and unhealthy dynamics. Expectations around constant availability and monitoring can lead to insecurity and mistrust, eroding the trust and freedom essential for a healthy partnership. Titles alone do not define the quality of a relationship. Instead, communication, trust, respect and mutual understanding truly shape its success. Navigating relationships with an open and empathetic mindset, where both partners are aware of their expectations and are willing to discuss and be flexible, can help foster healthier and more fulfilling connections. It's a reminder that titles and labels should reflect the depth of the relationship rather than a source of entitlement or control. In the journey of self-discovery, the *Say Yes to U* path encourages us to peel away the layers we've donned, like masks and titles and even the behaviors we feel entitled to because of these labels. It beckons us to explore who we truly are when we strip away these external identities. What happens when we summon the courage to reveal our genuine selves, unfiltered and untitled? And how do we handle the judgments that might come our way? The reality is that our titles often offer a superficial sense of security and belonging. They come with expectations and obligations that can feel almost like chains, but when we decide to cast aside these titles and exhibit our true essence, it can be unsettling.

We risk facing criticism and misunderstanding from others. In these moments, we tend to retreat back into our comfortable titles, seeking the safety of fitting in and feeling like we belong.

The journey of self-discovery is a dance between embracing our authenticity and confronting the fear of not being accepted. It asks us to prioritize our genuine selves over the need to conform or gain approval from the outside world. While it might be challenging, this journey ultimately leads to a deeper connection with ourselves and those who truly appreciate and accept us for who we are. It's a voyage of self-acceptance and self-love, where your well-being and happiness precede societal norms or others' expectations. You uncover your inner strength and beauty by embracing your authentic self. It's an ongoing adventure that leads to a more authentic and satisfying life.

When we shed these titles that, in reality, offer only a superficial sense of security, we uncover a fundamental question: Who are we at our core? It's perplexing how we can accumulate numerous titles in our lives, be it job positions, social statuses, or relationship labels and still feel a sense of emptiness. If these titles had the magical power to ensure perfect relationships and everlasting love, wouldn't the world be brimming with ideal connections? Yet, the harsh reality reveals a different story. Within the confines of these titles lie potential sources of misunderstanding, heartbreak and even scandal. These outcomes often sprout from the heavy burden of expectations tied to our titles. It's a recurring cycle of entitlement wherein we become obsessed with fulfilling societal norms and meeting the expectations linked to our roles. The fear of falling short of these standards looms like a dark cloud.

However, does our true worth genuinely hinge on these titles? Are we entitled to self-love and authentic fulfillment simply because of the roles we play or the labels we carry? The answer, of course, is a resounding no. Our intrinsic worth as individuals goes far beyond these external titles and should never be tethered to them.

True self-love and genuine fulfillment can only be discovered when we venture beyond the shallow realm of titles and explore the depths of our authentic selves. In our quest to understand how titles can foster a misguided sense of entitlement in our interactions with others, we should also turn the spotlight inward and examine our self-entitlement. Have we, perhaps unwittingly, adopted the belief that our titles or roles grant us a free pass to act without restraint, especially concerning ourselves? It's essential to recognize that this internalized sense of entitlement can profoundly impact our lives. As individuals, it's our responsibility to muster the courage needed to confront these entrenched beliefs and behaviors of entitlement that may have taken root within us. It's worth acknowledging that this learned behavior might have served a purpose for our grandparents and parents in their own time, perhaps as a means of survival or due to a lack of alternative options. However, we now stand on the precipice of a new era, determined to break free from these generational patterns. Our journey leads us down a different path that involves unraveling misunderstandings, healing long-held wounds and unlocking a treasure trove of inner tools. This inward exploration is the key to our personal growth and transformation. Breaking free from generational cycles requires embarking on an internal journey, delving deep into ourselves. It's within this profound inner exploration that healing takes root and its transformative effects ripple outward into our external experiences. To achieve this, we must summon the courage to confront the person we see in the mirror, approaching ourselves with compassion and self-acceptance and recognizing our pivotal role in shaping our lives.

A title is essentially a signpost guiding us in a particular direction or indicating our specific role. However, it is not a comprehensive representation of who we are. Beyond these titles, we are intricate and multifaceted beings, possessing depths that extend far beyond any label or societal expectation.

Therefore, it's time to wholeheartedly embrace our completeness, extending beyond the confines of titles. Our true worth and power aren't confined to the titles we hold. As we shed the cloak of entitlement, we open ourselves up to the boundless expanse of our being, inviting personal growth, transformation and a life that harmonizes with our deepest truths.

CHAPTER FOUR

The Judge

As I typed the word "Judge," a rush of emotions swept over me, unveiling the intricate web of our inherent judgmental tendencies. It's truly intriguing how deeply rooted this behavior is within us, quietly infiltrating our thoughts, behaviors and interactions. Armed with its reliable measurement yardstick, the Judge diligently scrutinizes and critiques every facet of our lives. Sometimes, we camouflage our judgments as opinions, convincing ourselves we have the right to hold and express them. After all, the diversity of perspectives is a fundamental aspect of human existence. However, there exists a delicate boundary between offering an opinion and passing judgment, which often blurs amid intense emotions. In their purest essence, opinions serve as subjective expressions of our thoughts, beliefs and experiences. They are reflections of our individuality, molded by a multitude of factors such as upbringing, culture and personal values. Opinions, when shared with respect and an open-minded spirit, have the potential to cultivate healthy dialogue. They can enhance our understanding of the world and contribute to personal growth. However, the transition from opinions to judgments signifies a shift in tone. Judgment, characterized by its critical undertones, aspires to classify, label and assess. It often imposes our standards and expectations onto others, establishing a hierarchical perspective. Judgment can be fueled by biases, preconceived notions and the desire to maintain control or superiority.

The challenge lies in recognizing when our opinions subtly transform into judgments, often without conscious awareness. We might catch ourselves making swift assessments of others based on superficial criteria or forming sweeping generalizations without considering their unique circumstances. The inner Judge can be overly eager, clouding our perception and impeding our ability to forge genuine connections and empathy. We must actively cultivate self-awareness and practice mindfulness to navigate this delicate balance. By tuning in to our thoughts and emotions, we can intercept ourselves in the act of passing judgments and intentionally pause for reflection. This involves asking ourselves if our opinions are grounded in factual evidence or if biases or unfounded assumptions tint them. Are we open to revising our perspectives when confronted with new information and alternative viewpoints?

Opinions are as abundant as grains of sand on a beach, each representing a unique viewpoint or judgment about a person, place, or thing. However, opinions aren't always rooted in fact or knowledge. They're a fusion of our perception and personal judgment, shaped by our experiences and beliefs. It's intriguing how we often misconstrue the nature of opinions, viewing them as an inherent right and a way to express our voices. Yet, they can be inherently biased, leading us to be judgmental. The line between expressing an opinion and passing judgment can become blurred as our biases and preconceived notions seep into our thoughts and color our perspectives.

We can succumb to judgmental behavior in various ways and it's important to acknowledge that it is a learned response. However, it is equally important to distinguish between being judgmental and being observant. While being observant entails being attentive, open-minded and seeking understanding, being judgmental leans toward making hasty assessments and clinging to rigid beliefs without considering all the facts. Observation is a powerful tool that allows us to perceive the world from a neutral standpoint. It enables us to gather information, analyze situations and gain deeper insights. On the other hand, judgment, deeply ingrained within us, manifests as an unhealthy behavior that negatively impacts our relationships with others and ourselves.

Can you recall a period in your own life when self-judgment consumed you? Every misstep and mistake became an opportunity to criticize and punish yourself. The cycle can seem never-ending: we judge ourselves, feel guilty, and then punish ourselves even further, creating a relentless cycle of self-destruction. The mirror becomes a battleground where we would scrutinize every inch of our being. Our stomachs are never flat enough, our body is not so perfect and the presence of minimal imperfections can become a source of deep dissatisfaction. We may feel we fell short of the ideal we set for ourselves. These thoughts can plague us incessantly, to the point where they become so ingrained that we are unaware of them or consider them the norm.

The effects of self-judgment can be profound and far-reaching. It chips away at our self-esteem, distorts our self-image and hinders our ability to embrace and appreciate ourselves fully. It robs us of the joy and acceptance we deserve, creating dissatisfaction and self-criticism. With its unrelenting focus on perfection, society has ingrained in us the notion that anything less than perfection is unacceptable and unworthy. It sets rigid standards for what is deemed acceptable beauty, leaving little room for individuality and diversity. Falling short of these societal ideals can result in fear, judgment and the relentless pursuit of fitting into a predetermined mold.

From a young age, growing up in the cult, the importance of appearances was instilled within us. We were expected to adhere to strict behavioral guidelines, constantly toeing the line of perfection. Stepping even an inch outside this predetermined path invited judgment, ridicule and the threat of ostracization. Though we may have disagreed with the judgments imposed upon us deep down, the pressure to conform eventually took its toll. In this environment of constant scrutiny and judgment, it became all too easy to turn the lens of judgment upon others and ourselves. No one wants to be in hell alone, after all. The fear of being ridiculed and embarrassed pushed us to participate in the very act of judgment we despised. As we internalize society's standards and judgments, we begin to view ourselves through the lens of perceived inadequacy. Our self-worth becomes entangled with meeting the impossible expectations set by others. We scrutinize our flaws, nitpicking every imperfection, convinced that they define our worth.

Let us challenge this notion. Let us question the validity of these external judgments and expectations. Who gets to determine what is beautiful, acceptable, or perfect? Can true beauty not be found in the unique tapestry of our individuality and authenticity? It is often said that women are among the most judgmental towards others and themselves. The pressure to appear perfect and have it all together has created an unhealthy divide within our sisterhood community. We find ourselves quick to pass judgment on other women, labeling and boxing them into categories based on our critical assessments. This behavior stems from the misguided belief that we have earned the right to judge others if we appear perfect. But does tearing someone else down truly make us feel good about ourselves? Does deriving satisfaction from putting others in their place elevate us? Upon closer examination, we may realize that our self-perceived elevation is not as genuine as we once thought.

The truth is that resorting to judgment to feel good about ourselves is a clear sign of insecurity and a lack of self-acceptance. It reveals a deep need for validation and an inability to find fulfillment within our own lives. In seeking to diminish others, we inadvertently diminish ourselves. However, let us not retreat into shame or hide from our judgmental tendencies. Instead, let us bring awareness to our actions and perspectives. Recognize that judgment is a learned behavior deeply ingrained in us, shaped by societal expectations and conditioning. Through this awareness, we can shift our perspective and behavior. By embracing empathy, compassion and a genuine desire to uplift one another, we can dismantle the harmful judgment cycle. Instead of tearing each other down, let us build each other up. Let us celebrate the diversity and uniqueness of every woman and human, under-standing that our differences are what makes us truly beautiful. In doing so, we foster an environ-ment of support, acceptance and love! We create a space where humans can freely express them-selves without fear of judgment. By lifting others, we elevate ourselves and contribute to a positive shift in the collective consciousness.

The fear of being negatively judged often serves as a mechanism to keep us in line with societal expectations. Our families, afraid of the potential judgment that may arise from their children's actions, strive to instill conformity to survive in a world that holds unrealistic and unfair standards. Breaking free from the grip of judgment is not an easy task. However, becoming aware of our judgmental tendencies towards others and ourselves can be a pivotal moment that prompts us to seek change. The discomfort that accompanies judgment, directed towards others and ourselves, clearly indicates that some-thing needs to shift.

This journey of self-transformation has not been without its challenges. The deeply ingrained nature of judgment makes breaking free from its grip difficult. Perhaps, even as you read these words, you may form judgments. However, it is important to understand that judgment only perpetuates a cycle of unhappiness and unfulfill-ment. It falsely convinces us that we are the ulti-mate arbiters of someone else's life and choices. Paradoxically, we become trapped by our fear of being judged, thus hindering our growth and self-expression.

The cycle of judgment keeps us confined, preventing us from experiencing true liberation and authenticity. By embracing acceptance and letting go of judgment, we allow ourselves and others the freedom to be who they truly are. We break free from the shackles of fear and create an environment of compassion, understanding and genuine connection. It is a continuous journey that requires self-reflection, self-compassion and a commitment to growth. Let us strive to release the judgment that holds us captive, both internally and externally. Remember, we are all on this journey together, learning and evolving.

The Power Of Healing

Healing is a profound process that we often approach when we are physically unwell yet shy away from when we feel that we are in good health. However, embarking on a healing journey is similar to peeling the layers of an onion—it can bring tears to our eyes. The layers of our conditioned existence have become so intertwined, relying on one another for support, that when we make the courageous decision to peel them back, a profound sense of relief washes over us. It is a relief from the weight of accumulated years that have bound our emotions and experiences within the layers of our being.

Although the benefits of healing are immense, many of us find ourselves evading it. We are afraid to face the depths of our wounds, even though we yearn for a life free from pain. It may not even be a conscious choice to run from healing; we may mistakenly believe that as long as we are not confined to a hospital bed or plagued by a severe illness, we are deemed "healthy." While it is true that we may possess a certain level of physical well-being, true healing or being healed encompasses something far more profound. True healing involves investigating the depths of our being, peeling back the layers that have accumulated over time. It requires acknowledging and addressing the emotional and spiritual wounds within us. It necessitates a willingness to confront our fears, traumas and limiting beliefs head-on. This transformative process empowers us to release what no longer serves us, cultivate self-compassion and forge a path toward wholeness.

The path to healing may be challenging and uncomfortable as we unravel long-held patterns and confront buried emotions. Yet, through this journey, we can truly experience profound growth, liberation and a sense of inner peace. Healing is not a destination, but a continual process of self-discovery, self-care and self-transformation. It is a sacred dance between our physical, emotional and spiritual selves; a harmonious integration that leads to a more authentic and vibrant existence. The first crucial step towards healing is acknowledging the presence of repressed pain within our emotional body.

However, it's understandable that looking into and healing something that appears old and insignificant may not be enticing. After all, you may have managed to survive for so long, enduring a few scratches, minor or major bruises and perhaps even some near-death experiences. The fact that you're still alive may lead you to believe that everything is fine, but is it truly well when unseen dark areas within your being remain unexplored?

Can we relate to being in denial when it comes to recognizing the existence of deep-rooted pain within us, or are we just afraid to confront it, to allow ourselves to feel and relive anything that we believe has caused us unnecessary suffering in our lives? Yet, as we continue to avoid the healing process, the pain persists. It's as if we have a wound that we either cover up with a bandage to hide or leave exposed while pretending it isn't painful. Eventually, we will realize that for the wound to heal, we must attend to it. Similarly, to experience healing, we must attend to the wounds within us. When we avoid healing, the pain remains trapped within us, influencing our thoughts, emotions and actions in subtle and often detrimental ways. It may manifest as self-sabotage, unhealthy coping mechanisms, or recurring patterns that prevent us from experiencing true joy and fulfillment. By avoiding the healing process, we inadvertently allow the pain to continue festering and affecting our overall well-being.

Acknowledging and embracing the need for healing is an act of self-compassion and empowerment. It is an invitation to honor our experiences, no matter how painful and to recognize that they have shaped us, but do not define us. By embarking on the healing journey, we allow ourselves to heal old wounds, release emotional baggage and cultivate a sense of wholeness and inner peace.

Take a moment to envision your 8-year-old self, residing in a household where singing and laughter are forbidden, despite your deep love for both. How would you navigate this innate desire to express yourself through singing and laughing? In such a restrictive environment, you would likely conceal that part of you, seeking solace in friends' homes or places where you could freely unleash your voice and laughter. Now, fast forward to the present, where you find yourself as an adult. The urge to sing and laugh still lingers within you, although it may have been suppressed over time. The conditioning and upbringing have instilled a fear of expressing these natural inclinations.

Consequently, you carry a burden of resentment towards your family, coupled with guilt and shame for resenting them due to their adherence to their own rules. Remarkably, you have now become an adult who inhibits others from fully expressing themselves in any capacity. This perpetuates a cycle of pain and other undesirable attributes that contribute to its continuation. It becomes evident how suppressing our authentic selves can have far-reaching consequences. When we are prevented from embracing and expressing our true nature, we may experience a sense of disconnection from ourselves and others. The longing to be seen, heard and accepted becomes a silent ache that echoes within us. Therefore, deep within us, feelings buried alive never truly fade away; instead, they ferment and multiply, creating a putrid essence within our being. Like the stench of rotting matter, these unaddressed emotions emit an undesirable aura that permeates our lives. Nobody willingly seeks out the scent of decay or consumes spoiled food. Yet, we walk around carrying this internal rottenness; a pain that influences and perpetuates unhealthy behaviors toward others and ourselves.

Recognizing the presence of this rotten pain is a vital step towards healing. It is an acknowledgment that something within us requires attention and resolution. As I pour my thoughts into this book, I am reminded of my journey, experiencing various levels of healing. Healing is not a one-time event; it unfolds gradually, revealing itself in different stages and phases throughout our lives. However, the crucial aspect is that we must actively invite and embrace the healing process; it will not impose itself upon us. Imagine the relief of letting go of the burden of rotten pain, of purging the toxicity that has accumulated within. By facing our deepest wounds and addressing the lingering emotions associated with them, we open the door to profound healing. Just like the cycles of nature, our healing journey evolves, offering us opportunities for growth and self-discovery. It requires us to be gentle with ourselves to nurture our wounds with kindness and understanding.

As I embarked on my healing journey, little did I know that it would extend far beyond my expectations. It all began with a challenging divorce that shook the very foundation of my being. The prospect of being on my own again filled me with fear, especially considering that I now had the responsibility of caring for my two precious children. The aftermath of the divorce took a toll on my confidence and spirit, leaving me feeling lost and uncertain. I was a stay-at-home mom during that period, seemingly living my best life. We were constructing a magnificent nine-bedroom house on 16 acres of picturesque land with a gently flowing creek. It was a dream setting many would envy, but strangely enough, it didn't bring me the fulfillment I sought. While my material and physical needs were well catered for, there was a deep void within that couldn't be satisfied by material possessions alone. I had become overly reliant on my parents and close friends' opinions and guidance regarding my relationship. When things turned sour between my ex-husband and me, I blamed them for their trusted input.

During this tumultuous time, the seeds of my healing journey were sown. I realized that true healing required me to take ownership of my own life and decisions. Throughout this ongoing healing journey, I have encountered numerous challenges and triumphs. It hasn't been a linear progression, but rather a winding path filled with ups and downs. It dawned on me that perhaps I had been living in a state of ignorance, unaware of my true self and lacking clarity about my desires. Following my divorce, as I approached my 27th birthday, I consciously decided to infuse spiritual intention into my celebration. I wanted to reflect on my past mistakes, creating a path of clarity for my present and future journey. Surrounded by my dear friends and family, I held a small ceremony where I made a heartfelt commitment to be intentional in my choices and actions moving forward.

Little did I realize the profound depth of what lay ahead on this newfound road. The journey towards authenticity and intentionality required me to embark on a path of healing. I must admit the idea of healing initially evoked fear within me. I was uncertain about what would surface during the process. However, I soon came to understand that healing is not an instantaneous event. It unfolds gradually, gently revealing layers of wounds and unhealed aspects of ourselves. In truth, it is unfair to expect immediate healing, considering that the wounds we carry have accumulated over time. The initial phase of healing often involves attributing blame to others for our pain, such as our parents. During this stage, we begin to find our adult voice, becoming conscious of the influence our parents had on us and summoning the courage to rebel against their indoctrination. We stand up for our inner being, slowly recollecting the moments in our childhood when we longed to express ourselves, but could not do so. In this process, we may confront our parents, expressing to them the ways in which they fell short or caused us harm.

This cycle of communication and confrontation may continue as we uncover more about our parents, ourselves and our personal journey. However, it is important to remember that this is just the beginning.

From then to now, my healing journey continues to unfold. There are periods when I find myself preoccupied with other aspects of life, making prioritizing or inviting healing difficult. And then, there are times when life compels me to pause, allowing me the opportunity to confront the healing that needs to take place. There will be moments when we are actively engaged in the healing process and there will be moments when we unintentionally set it aside. Each stage of life presents us with different circumstances and opportunities for growth. Through these experiences, healing becomes interwoven into our existence. As I continue on my healing journey, I am aware of the ongoing nature of this process. I am learning to embrace the times of stillness and introspection, recognizing that they provide fertile ground for healing to occur. I also acknowledge the moments when life pulls me in different directions, understanding that healing may take a backseat during those periods.

Judgment is a significant obstacle to our healing journey. Initiating the healing process becomes difficult if we constantly judge ourselves and others. The unconscious tendency to judge and self-punish for past and ongoing mistakes hinders our ability to acknowledge and address unresolved and unhealed aspects of ourselves. This perpetual cycle keeps us concealed, driven by fear and shame. We often reassure ourselves that we are fine just the way we are, but reflecting on the concept of mistakes is crucial. A mistake only remains as such if we consistently fail to grasp the lessons embedded within our experiences. Otherwise, it is merely an opportunity for growth and learning. If we repeatedly overlook the gentle nudges from the universe, nudges guiding us towards healing and transformation, we impede our progress. On the path of healing, we must cultivate empathy and compassion towards ourselves. It is important to recognize that we did not consciously choose this version of ourselves; it was imposed upon us. We carry the weight of past experiences and conditioning circumstances that have shaped us. Embracing empathy allows us to acknowledge our inherent worthiness of healing and grants us permission to confront our wounds with kindness and understanding.

We create an environment conducive to healing by relinquishing judgment and cultivating self-compassion. We liberate ourselves from the burdens of self-blame and shame. Healing becomes a transformative journey, an act of reclaiming our authentic selves and embracing the profound power of self-love. As we extend compassion towards ourselves, we also extend it to others. Recognizing that each person carries their burdens and battles allows us to approach them with empathy instead of judgment. This shift in perspective fosters deeper connections, understanding and collective healing. We often turn to God/ Universe and make requests, seeking answers and guidance.

Surprisingly, life always responds, but frequently, we fail to recognize the answer. It lies in the realm of healing, an aspect many of us fear to engage with, causing us to live unhealed lives and experience a sense of unfulfillment. Healing is an ever-present companion on our journey, one that requires courage and trust to embrace fully. I resisted healing consistently, desiring it to conform to my comfort level. However, after sixteen years, I have developed a profound appreciation, respect and love for the transformative power of healing. When we grant ourselves the courage and permission to invite healing into our lives, we witness a profound transformation unfolding. Healing holds the key to unlocking the dormant potential within us. It is through healing that we shed the layers of pain, past traumas and emotional burdens that hinder our growth. By facing these wounds head-on, we begin to experience the true power of healing. It is a journey that requires us to be vulnerable, to delve into the depths of our being and to trust the process.

As we embark on this courageous path, our lives undergo a remarkable metamorphosis. We witness the gradual unraveling of old patterns, the dissipation of emotional baggage and the emergence of our authentic selves.

Through healing, we understand our strength, resilience and capacity for growth. It is a profound act of self-love and self-empowerment. Therefore, I urge you to grant yourself permission to embrace healing. Trust in its transformative potential and open yourself to its gentle touch. As you do so, observe how your life begins to shift and transform in ways you never imagined. Embrace the journey, for it is through healing that we awaken to our true selves and find the fulfillment we seek.

The Caterpillar Is The Butterfly

As we undergo the remarkable transformation from caterpillar to butterfly, it is easy to overlook the significance of our humble beginnings. The caterpillar, often dismissed as a plain and slow-moving worm, serves as the vessel that nurtures us during our darkest hours of transformation. Yet, in our newfound beauty as a butterfly, we sometimes forget the essential role the caterpillar played in our journey. Consider the process the caterpillar undergoes within its cocoon. It is a profound metamorphosis, comparable to the journey of a sperm racing towards an egg and then developing over nine months in the mother's womb. We eagerly anticipate the arrival of a newborn, wondering what they will look like and who they will become. We embrace the process of creation, patiently or impatiently awaiting this bundle of joy.

In this process, the baby is blissfully unaware of its transformation. Similarly, the butterfly emerges from its cocoon, possibly unaware of the extraordinary journey it has experienced. Both the baby and the butterfly embody the miracle of transformation, a testament to the intricate cycles of life. The caterpillar teaches us the importance of embracing our humble beginnings and recognizing the value of each stage of our journey. It reminds us that growth and beauty can arise from the most unassuming places. Just as the butterfly evolves from the caterpillar, we, too, undergo countless cycles of growth, shedding old layers to reveal our true essence. We are constantly evolving, even when we may not know the depth of our transformation. The caterpillar and the butterfly are not separate entities, but interconnected aspects of the same extraordinary journey.

It is often observed that many aspire to be graceful butterflies while overlooking the inherent beauty of the caterpillar. They shy away from embracing the caterpillar as if it does not deserve admiration equally. Yet, the process of transformation itself is a remarkable and wondrous journey. Through this journey of unapologetically saying *Yes* to oneself, with *no F's given,* that true beauty unfolds. To become a butterfly, one must wholeheartedly embrace all aspects of oneself, including the caterpillar. It is crucial to recognize the beauty and value inherent in every stage of transformation. How can one fully appreciate the magnificence of the butterfly if one cannot appreciate the humble beginnings of the caterpillar?

Transformation can be intimidating, as much of it occurs in the darkness. Not only are we often afraid of the dark, but we also fear confronting our own inner shadows. However, it is within this darkness, within the cocoon of our being, that profound transformation takes place. In this cocoon, we are faced with a choice: to be a witness to the magnificent unfolding or to remain in denial, only relishing the anticipation of becoming a butterfly. True beauty lies not just in the final form, but also in the process itself. The caterpillar represents a stage of growth and preparation, an essential part of the transformative journey. By embracing and honoring every stage, we open ourselves up to the fullness of our potential.

Why do we feel ashamed of the essence that has shaped us into who we are today, regardless of its nature? Why do we rush to become the butterfly, disregarding the value of the caterpillar stage? What truly resonates within us, driving our thirst for transformation? Society has conditioned us to believe that only glitter signifies gold, that only sparkle signifies diamonds and that lacking financial wealth equates to poverty. Is this how we perceive the caterpillar as lacking value? Is this why we feel shame for the scars that accompany us on our journey?

Why do we yearn to be anything other than

ourselves? Why do we consider the parts of ourselves unattractive or unacceptable and unworthy? How have we allowed societal conditioning to convince us that life made a mistake in creating us? Look at the caterpillar—life made no mistakes in its transformation into a butterfly.

You, as a soul, are extraordinary and inherently perfect, just as you were on the day of your birth. There is no need to feel ashamed of your existence. However, perfection does not preclude transformation. Remember that you have become a product of your environment and within you lies the patient potential to blossom and align with the original purpose of your design. Everything in your life is intricately designed; you only need to awaken from the cocoon of conditioning. Embrace the essence that has molded you, for it has shaped your unique journey. Embrace the beauty in both the caterpillar and the butterfly, recognizing their equal significance. Let go of societal judgments and honor your true self. You are a magnificent being, destined to unfurl your wings and embrace the fullness of your transformation.

Life has its share of pain, but surprisingly, the potential for bliss and joy lies within that pain. It may be hard to believe, but there is a profound truth in the saying that pain is enveloped within the shell of our understanding. When we embark on the journey of examining and exploring our pain, we gradually realize that much of it stems from misunderstandings. In this process of self-exploration, we discover that the caterpillar does not envy the butterfly because it is, in fact, the transformed form of the caterpillar itself. Similarly, as human beings, we possess an incredible capacity for self-transformation. We can heal our wounds, embrace our shadows and accept our pain.

As we delve deeper into understanding our misunderstandings and the lenses through which we perceive the world and ourselves, we witness a profound transformation before our eyes.

By embracing our pain and seeking clarity, we tap into the inherent beauty of the human experience. We become active participants in our own metamorphosis. Through this transformative process, we not only find healing, but also discover the profound wisdom and resilience that lies within us. As we shed the layers of misunderstanding and embrace our authentic selves, we open ourselves to a world of joy, fulfillment and boundless possibilities. Transformation is not only a process that can be painful at times, but it also requires a deep sense of trust in both our own capacity for change and in the larger forces of life. When we observe the journey of the caterpillar as it transforms into a butterfly, we witness a beautiful illustration of surrendering to the natural flow of transformation. The caterpillar doesn't anxiously peek out of the cocoon every few days, eagerly checking if it has become a butterfly. Instead, it embraces trust in the process and allows life to guide its metamorphosis.

Similarly, many of us carry a lack of trust within ourselves and in the unfolding of life. Our past experiences of trauma, abuse, betrayal and deception have left us doubtful and unsure of what to believe. It's a natural response to such circumstances. I personally understand this struggle, as it took me years to learn how to trust this process and, most importantly, to trust myself.

If we desire to live a life filled with joy, it is essential that we cultivate trust in our hearts and in the inner voice that guides us. However, before we can fully embrace this trust, we must first peel away the layers of pain and misunderstanding that shroud our true essence. We must enter our metaphorical cocoon, where healing, transformation and surrender take place to the process with patience and acceptance. Transformation does not happen overnight. It requires time, nurturing and the willingness to let go of what no longer serves us. As we gradually remove the barriers that hinder trust, we begin to tap into our inherent wisdom and intuition. We rediscover our innate ability to navigate life's twists and turns, guided by an unwavering faith in our transformational journey. Trust becomes a powerful ally on this path, allowing us to surrender to the natural flow of life, embrace the unknown and ultimately experience the profound joy that comes from aligning with our authentic selves.

CHAPTER FIVE

The Blues of Always and Never

Gratitude, often practiced at the surface level, can be a subtle art. When we limit our thankfulness to the obvious blessings, we miss out on the deeper, less apparent aspects of life that warrant our appreciation. So, what's the true measure of gratitude? It's a journey of unlearning the ingrained habit of taking things for granted and relearning the profound art of genuine appreciation for life's every facet. Let's be real here. Unlearning is a tough nut to crack, just as challenging as the initial learning itself. The intriguing part lies in the distinction between the two. When we learn to conform, it often happens without our conscious awareness.

We simply see it as a means of survival, a ticket to fitting in and never as a deviation from the norm. However, unlearning demands a conscious acknowledgment that there's some unraveling. Picture a tightly woven fabric that makes up our current existence. We must delicately unpick each thread to undo it, one painstaking step at a time. Cultivating an attitude of gratitude is where the real magic happens. It's an invitation to the profound change and transformation we often yearn for, but might be hesitant to embrace. Gratitude isn't a quick fix; it's a gentle process that allows us to embrace the undoing of old patterns, even if it's not easy. But here's the thing: it's incredibly powerful and can bring about profound change. To truly set forth on your *Say Yes To U* journey, it's crucial to acknowledge the challenges ahead and recognize gratitude's pivotal role in this process. Without it, it's as if we're standing still at the starting line, trapped in idealistic visions of how life should be. These ideals can shackle our personal growth, keeping us fixated on desires and preventing us from fully embracing the present moment's reality.

In this context, we encounter two significant roadblocks: the influence of absolutes and our tendency to believe in "always" and "never." These words often slip into our language when we're trying to express dissatisfaction, but in reality, they only feed our discontent. You might find yourself trapped in the "Always and Never" syndrome, particularly within relationships. Phrases like "you always leave your clothes on the floor" or "you never tell me you love me" become all too familiar.

But here's the truth: nobody is truly capable of always doing the exact same thing every time. Life is beautifully fluid and ever-evolving. Similarly, sweeping "never" statements can't encapsulate the intricacies of human behavior. When we acknowledge the limitations of absolutes, we break free from the never-ending cycle of complaints and open ourselves to understanding the nuances of life and human nature. The words "always" and "never" can indeed cast a shadow over our relationships, closing us off to the nuances of life. They limit our understanding and prevent us from embracing the shades of grey that make our experiences rich and complex. Instead of seeing life as a combination of 'sometimes,' we get trapped in the absolutes, failing to recognize the ebb and flow of existence.

It's vital to realize that not every need or desire can be fulfilled by external sources. Struggle, challenges and moments of lack are essential for our growth and development. When we overly rely on the terms "always" and "never," we unknowingly cultivate an attitude of unappreciation and disregard the reality of our situation. In its wisdom, life provides us with what we need, considering our capabilities and what we believe and know we truly deserve. Living authentically is the key to truly appreciating life's offerings. Every twist and turn, whether it leads to success or challenge, is a piece of the intricate puzzle that makes us who we are. Our experiences, both pleasant and trying, mirror the desires of our hearts and guide us toward our life's purpose. By letting go of rigid "always" and "never" thinking, we allow ourselves to bask in the tapestry of "sometimes," finding gratitude in every step of our transformation. In this revelation, I've come to understand that my role is to be present for myself and give my all in every situation. Along the way, there will be stumbles, mistakes, heartbreaks and losses, but each serves as a valuable lesson. Learning becomes the thread that runs through the fabric of life. Shifting our focus away from what we lack and shedding the belief that life owes us our every desire allows us to embrace the beauty in falling and rising through the process of learning and growth.

Every obstacle in life is like a wake-up call, urging us to rise and embrace transformation. It might sting, even causing pain or injury, but it demands our presence, nudging us to be grateful for the here and now. Gratitude is a critical companion on this journey, preventing us from replaying the same patterns. Let's refrain from sizing up our lives through the narrow lenses of "always" and "never." Life is a constant provider, always delivering in its unique way, but we must remain vigilant. Gratitude is our guide, rescuing us from the cycle of repetition and leading us toward a path where we continually learn, grow and cherish the ever-unfolding journey. I believe that life sends challenges our way to test our gratitude meter. Confronting these hurdles provides an opportunity to prove our mettle and see how adept we are at surmounting the toughest obstacles. Interestingly, once we conquer a daunting challenge, it loses its intimidation factor and we gain the wisdom and experience needed to surpass it. Certainly, life's challenges play a crucial role in shaping our character and nurturing our resilience. If everything were readily available and effortless, we might become disengaged, lacking the motivation to push ourselves further. Adversity serves as a catalyst for growth, prompting us to confront our limitations and strive for personal excellence. It instills within us a sense of humility and perseverance, allowing us to appreciate the value of hard-earned achievements. Genuine gratitude transcends mere recognition of favorable circumstances. It encompasses an understanding of the transformative power embedded within life's trials and tribulations. When we adopt this mindset, we begin to perceive challenges as opportunities for self-discovery and personal evolution. This shift in perspective enables us to embrace the entirety of our journey, recognizing both the highs and lows as essential components of our ongoing development. Initially, our experiences of gratitude may have been superficial, reflecting a surface-level understanding of life's blessings. As we mature and accumulate life experiences, our capacity for profound gratitude deepens, reflecting the wisdom and insights gained along the way.

Growing up in a cult, the ritual of praying five times daily felt like an overwhelming chore. Each call to prayer reverberated through the walls, disrupting my playtime and evoking a sense of aversion. Prayer became more of a mechanical duty rather than a heartfelt connection. This discord followed me into adulthood, breeding a deep-seated resentment towards spirituality and religious practices. It wasn't until life presented me with its share of challenges and close calls that I began to seek solace in my own spiritual journey. Exploring my spiritual path, I realized that my prayers and spiritual practices had been merely superficial, reserved for moments of distress when I sought a quick fix. Even when my prayers were answered, my gratitude felt insincere, raising doubts about the true purpose of my spiritual practices.

This realization is part of the unfolding process, which encompasses a complex tapestry of intertwined experiences that have shaped our being. Years of conditioning have kept us living on the surface, hesitant to go deep for fear of drowning. However, what we fail to recognize is that by staying on the surface, we are slowly suffocating and this is far unhealthier. By the time we realize we have been gradually drowning, it may be too late to make the profound changes that are necessary for our lives. Acknowledging this perspective, we are invited to confront our fears and dive into the depths of our being. It is in these uncharted waters that true transformation occurs. We must learn to let go of the safety of the surface and explore the richness and expansiveness that lie within.

Both surface-level and genuine gratitude have their place in our lives, as each serves a purpose in our journey of change, growth and transformation. It is essential for us to recognize and acknowledge the distinction between the two, allowing us to cultivate and invite genuine gratitude into our lives. We must understand that life itself is the creator of this magnificent masterpiece called human beings and it has intricately designed every aspect of our existence. It is perfectly all right to admit that our gratitude may sometimes lack authenticity. This awareness enables us to discern and embrace the genuine moments of gratitude that arise within us. Now, I want to clarify that I am not an expert in gratitude or life itself and I certainly don't possess all the answers for my life or yours. However, the information I share from my experience serves as a tool that can dismantle what no longer serves us and incorporate what is best to continue our journey.

Understanding this process can be challenging because we often believe that practicing gratitude will guarantee a consistently smooth life. However, that is not the case. Life is a continuous implementation and maintenance process and we need to learn how to access the tools that allow our lives to flow. Through self-awareness, introspection and utilizing these tools, we can navigate the ups and downs, fostering a deeper sense of gratitude and finding harmony amidst the ever-changing tides of life.

Gratitude is an essential tool on our journey and genuine gratitude specifically connects us to our inner world. It allows us to cultivate a deep reverence for life, recognizing that it holds ultimate control and that we must learn to flow with its rhythm. When we struggle to accept life's dance and its inherent rhythm, resentment can take hold, hindering our ability to practice gratitude.

Perhaps our struggle stems from our understanding of free will. We have been taught that we have the power to make choices and indeed we do. However, we must also recognize the limits of our free will and acknowledge that life itself possesses its own free will. Finding the balance between our personal agency and surrendering to the greater flow of life is vital to practicing gratitude.

In truth, the most crucial starting point for gratitude is simply being grateful for the gift of being alive. This realization should be enough to ignite our journey towards gratitude. After all, we all share the desire to live a fulfilling and meaningful life for as long as possible. And in that desire, practicing gratitude becomes paramount. As we continue to navigate life's journey, we will inevitably encounter turbulent tides. These moments serve as reminders that we are truly alive and they further emphasize the importance of embracing gratitude as a guiding force on our path.

CHAPTER SIX

Feel The Feelings

Nobody willingly seeks out experiences or consequences that cause us pain, rejection, or disappointment. It has become a central mission in our lives to evade these perceived negative emotions at all costs. Yet, ironically, our attempts to avoid pain often fall short as we inevitably encounter it. This paradox raises an intriguing question: Could it be that to live truly, we must experience pain at some point? Could pain catalyze growth and transformation? Consider the remarkable example of birth itself. Both the mother and the child experience pain during the birthing process. The mother is conscious of and remembers the pain, while the newborn remains unaware of the mother's experience. However, the infant also undergoes its own form of pain as it navigates the transition from the comfort and stillness of the womb to the external world. This process, known as contractions, involves stretching and repositioning. Perhaps this ebb and flow, this constant process of change and adaptation, is mirrored throughout our entire lives.

From the moment of birth, we may have missed a crucial lesson: that life itself can be a painful process. If we were unable to feel pain, how could we truly experience or understand love? It is through the contrast of pain and pleasure, hardship and joy, that we gain a deeper appreciation for the profound moments of connection, love and fulfillment. A few years ago, when I was teaching the *Say Yes to U* 9-week course, I had the opportunity to work with a group of seven women who enrolled and completed the nine-week program. Out of those participants, four of them actively took part in their final *Say Yes To U* ceremony. It was during this transformative journey that I came to recognize the profound importance of feelings and emotions.

To my surprise, many of the women in the program were disconnected from their true feelings. They had been living under the illusion that their thoughts and emotions represented their feelings, but I soon discovered that it was not the complete picture. In order to address this, I introduced the concept of creating a feelings board, which allowed them to explore and express their emotions and feelings more effectively.

What struck me the most was that every

woman in the program shared a common desire: to avoid getting hurt and to shield themselves from experiencing pain once again. Their past stories were filled with shame, disappointment, abuse, rejection and abandonment, all of which had culminated in pain. It seemed that in our efforts to avoid pain, we inadvertently focused only on the negative and painful aspects of our personal narratives.

But why is that? Why do we tend to fixate on the seemingly negative and painful parts of our stories? It became evident to me that we often cling to a small fraction of pain that remains unresolved within us. This unresolved pain acts as a magnet, attracting more painful experiences into our lives. It is a consequence of our limited understanding of the complex nature of emotions and how they can disguise themselves.

By delving into our emotions and allowing ourselves to fully experience them, we gain a deeper understanding of ourselves and our past. We can begin the process of healing and resolving unresolved pain, thereby breaking the cycle of attracting more pain into our lives. It is through this journey of self-discovery and emotional exploration that we can truly transform and create a more fulfilling and joyful existence.

So, in the *Say Yes to U* course, we placed great emphasis on recognizing and acknowledging our feelings, unraveling the layers of pain and ultimately finding healing and empowerment. By embracing the entirety of our emotional landscape, we can move forward with greater self-awareness, authenticity and resilience. Our feelings are indeed crucial, regardless of whether they are positive, negative, or neutral. Each emotion holds significance because every individual and their feelings matter. Denying ourselves the right to feel and acknowledge our emotions is a grave injustice. In fact, it can be considered the greatest offense, the most significant harm we can inflict upon ourselves. I, too, had developed a habit of suppressing my feelings. In situations where someone hurt me, I would often present a false sense of understanding, masking the fact that deep down, my feelings were hurt, or I felt disappointed. I would fail to express myself authentically and if I did decide to convey my true emotions, it would often be in an unhealthy and harmful manner, unintentionally inflicting pain upon the other person. This pattern perpetuated a cycle of denial, preventing me from truly embracing and honoring my feelings, but this is the reality we must confront. We cannot genuinely Say Yes to ourselves if we continue to live in a bubble of safety and denial. This belief and behavior undermine our sense of self-worth and prevent us from acknowledging that our feelings matter. If we fail to recognize our emotions as valid and important, how can we expect others to treat us authentically and respectfully? It is through the way we treat ourselves that we communicate to others how they should treat us.

Navigating the realm of expressing our

emotions can indeed be complex. While it is essential to acknowledge and understand our feelings, it is equally important to recognize that others are not responsible for how we feel. In my own experience, I realized that blaming others for my insecurities, dissatisfaction, or disappointment only perpetuated more dissatisfaction. The truth is, no one else can change how we feel about ourselves or alter our perception of the world around us. This realization challenges one of the biggest misconceptions ingrained in society. While there are instances when it is necessary to communicate our emotions and concerns, it is equally valuable to sit with our feelings and gain deeper self-awareness.

It is important to remember that others may be unaware of their own emotions and feelings. Therefore, they can only share, say, or give from their inner world and understanding. They cannot be held responsible for our unresolved emotions or dissatisfaction. Just as we have been shaped by our own experiences and beliefs, so have they. When we find ourselves attributing our unresolved feelings to others, it is crucial to remember that we are all on a similar journey of acknowledging and expressing our authentic emotions.

In this process, we can draw inspiration from the serenity prayer: "God grant me the serenity to change the things that I can, the courage to accept the things that I cannot change and the wisdom to know the difference." It reminds us that we have the power to change ourselves and our responses, but we cannot change others. By focusing on our growth and understanding, we create a space for empathy and compassion toward others who are also navigating their emotional landscapes. Ultimately, by taking responsibility for our feelings and recognizing that others have their journeys, we can cultivate healthier relationships and foster a deeper understanding of ourselves and those around us. It is a continuous process of self-reflection, self-compassion and open heartedness as we embrace the shared struggle of acknowledging and expressing our authentic feelings.

Pain As A Teacher

As you glance at the subtitle of this chapter, you may find yourself questioning the notion that pain can serve as a teacher. Isn't the purpose of life to seek joy and avoid pain at all costs? Who willingly chooses pain as their teacher? Trust me, I understand. I, like you, went to great lengths to evade pain, clinging to the belief that if I followed all the right steps in life, I could safeguard myself from its grasp. We all yearn for a life where we can have our cake and eat it, too, don't we?

In our pursuit of happiness, pain often gets pushed aside and labeled as an unwanted guest. We diligently construct walls and barriers to shield ourselves from its touch. Yet, as you embark on this chapter, I invite you to consider a profound perspective: pain can be an unexpected teacher, a catalyst for growth and transformation.

Although it may seem counterintuitive, the pain has a remarkable ability to reveal truths, deepen our understanding and awaken dormant strength within us. It holds valuable lessons that shape our character, expand our resilience and redefine our perspectives. Society has conditioned us to believe that life should be devoid of pain. However, I invite you to consider this: without the ability to feel pain, we would also lose the capacity to truly experience life in its entirety. Pain serves as a vital receptor, signaling that adjustments or healing are needed, both physically, emotionally and spiritually.

There's a saying that "pain is weakness leaving the body", but I see it differently. I believe pain is more like a conditioning misunderstanding. As children, many of us were discouraged from expressing our authentic thoughts and feelings. We were labeled as disobedient if we dared to challenge the norm. This conditioning caused us pain because going against ourselves meant going against the very essence of life and the universe that created us to be unique individuals. Over time, this conditioning has led us astray from our authentic selves. We have become detached from the core of who we are. However, there is beauty in the midst of this unresolved pain. It serves as a powerful teacher, guiding us back to the true essence of our being that we may have buried in order to navigate a world that often rejects authenticity. Indeed, pain is a remarkable teacher, one that I have come to appreciate deeply on my journey. When I initially embarked on this path of self-discovery, I didn't anticipate encountering pain along the way. I naively believed that as long as I acknowledged myself, made peace with my past and recited a few positive affirmations to myself, everything would be smooth sailing. Little did I know that true healing often requires us to delve into the depths of our pain. Think about it. When we accidentally burn ourselves, it stings and the pain lingers until we tend to the wound. As we apply medication and care, the pain subsides, but then it resurfaces in stages during the healing process. It may itch and form new skin, leaving behind a scar as a tangible reminder of the past pain that occurred and has now healed. This scar serves as a gentle caution, reminding us to be cautious when we come into contact with hot tools or stoves in the future. Pain, in this sense, becomes a beautiful process—a teacher that guides us toward greater awareness.

Similarly, our emotional pain follows a similar trajectory. It demands our attention, urging us to confront and address the unresolved wounds within us. By acknowledging and allowing ourselves to fully experience our pain, we open the door to profound healing and growth. Through the transformative power of embracing our pain, we can release the weight of the past and cultivate resilience and strength. It is through this process that we learn valuable lessons about ourselves, our relationships and our place in the world.

As we open ourselves to listen and acknowledge the pain within, a remarkable transformation begins to unfold. Gradually, we reconnect with our authentic core, our genuine love and it is nothing short of magical and magnificent. It's true that along this journey, we may encounter emotional battle wounds and scars, but they serve as a testament to our healing and growth. They remind us of the depth and capacity of our ability to love authentically, which is the very thing we yearn for.

Consider the timeless adage, "No pain, no gain." There is inherent truth in those words. What have we truly gained if we haven't experienced loss or undergone transformation? The unconscious pain of losing ourselves has burdened us throughout our lives. We searched for fulfillment everywhere, in others, in external pursuits, only to be left with a lingering sense of emptiness. Pain becomes our trusted teacher, guiding us to the areas where we have emotional and spiritual deficiencies. Just as physical and mental well-being are important, so are the realms of emotion and spirituality.

Through this process, we gain a profound understanding of ourselves, uncovering the depths of our emotions and forging a profound connection with our spiritual essence. Keep in mind your very birth was a process fraught with pain, even though you may not recall it. Yet, once you embark on healing from your unconscious, unresolved pain, a world of profound joy, gratitude, love and so much more awaits you. You will taste the very essence of life itself, the embodiment of who you truly are. The creation of this book emerged from the depths of my own unresolved pain. The anguish of losing custody of my children, the heartbreak of parting ways with my best friend and love of my life, the sorrow of ending long-term friendships. Each experience was accompanied by its own unique brand of pain, but I reached a point where I could no longer evade or escape it.

You see, I am the common thread in all my relationships and if I continue to encounter pain and loss, then perhaps the answers lie within. I had to muster the courage to delve inward to embark on a transformative journey of self-discovery and healing. I needed to take those pivotal steps towards introspection, embracing the pain as a catalyst for change and becoming the embodiment of the transformation I yearned for. In this book, I share my personal testament of saying "yes" to myself— the triumphs, the setbacks and the profound lessons learned along the way. It is my sincere hope that by exploring my own healing process, you, too, will find inspiration, guidance and the motivation to embark on your transformative path.

Remember, you are not alone in your pain. By delving deep within and facing your unresolved pain with courage and self-compassion, you can unlock the boundless potential within you. Embrace the power of saying "yes" to yourself, for it is through this self-empowerment that you can truly be the change you wish to see in the world. So, as we explore the profound nature of pain and its role as a teacher, let us release our preconceived notions and judgments and let us embrace the opportunity to learn from our pain and rekindle our authenticity. Pain is not an enemy to be feared, but rather a guide that leads us back to the truth of who we are.

The Art Of Saying Yes To U

S aying yes to yourself might come off as cliché, even a bit cheesy, but let me tell you, it's as real as it gets. At least, it's real in my world. When I embarked on my journey of saying yes to me, I had no roadmap, no GPS guiding me. All I knew was that I was standing at a crossroads, needing a seismic shift in my life. I was drowning in an overwhelming sea, like pouring my heart and soul into everyone else's cup while mine ran dry.

Growing up, I was handed a script: "Be a good girl, serve God and mankind!" The storyline was etched in stone: school, high school diploma, college maybe, marriage, kids and voila, ride off into the sunset, but life, well, it's got its plot twists. It decided to take me on a rollercoaster instead. I found myself not completing school, married and then unmarried, juggling financial burdens, another failed relationship and facing the gut punch of feeling completely adrift, a certified failure in my own eyes. You see, the comparison bug is a bit hard. I let it nest in my thoughts. "Not good enough," it hissed. So, there I was, letting this idea gnaw at my self-worth, all because I wasn't ticking boxes on society's checklist. And man, this mentality rob me blind! But as I tiptoed into the realm of saying yes to myself, something magical unfolded. It was like a veil lifting. Slowly, I started to unchain myself from these expectations. I realized that to truly appreciate everything around me, I had to start with appreciating myself. It's as if learning to say yes to me became the skeleton key that unlocked a treasure trove of self-love and authenticity. It wasn't about rebelling against norms, but rather about carving out my niche of happiness.

The power of saying yes to yourself is akin to the process of death and rebirth. When you intentionally commit to putting yourself first, your heart, your genuine essence, you start seeing the world for what it truly is, not just through the filter of your desires.

This transformational journey, however, isn't always a walk in the park. Our minds and bodies are wired to believe that life should cater to our every whim, but here's the twist: life isn't just a vending machine for our wants. It's a dynamic, unpredictable force. When you embrace this truth, you're on the brink of a significant shift. Life gives ceaselessly; it's in every breath you take, every moment you're alive. Even engaging with these words is a manifestation of life, giving you a chance to explore thoughts and ideas. It's admittedly not the easiest notion to digest or put into practice. Yet, as you diligently say yes to yourself, your heart and the very essence of life, you begin to witness change. It's like a ripple effect, starting from within and touching every aspect of your existence. It's about allowing yourself to embrace each day's miracle and cherish the gift of life that's bestowed upon you. As you practice this, your reality takes on new hues and your journey becomes a testament to the transformative power of saying yes to you.

You owe yourself the unapologetic affirmation to say yes to you with absolute disregard for the opinions of others, living your life with an unabashed attitude of *No F*cks Given*. Throughout your existence, you've inadvertently downplayed and devalued yourself to fit into the mold expected by society, all to avoid being labeled as a rebel or an outlier. But even while trying to conform, you're inevitably judged for your actions, whether they're deemed right or wrong according to external standards, much like how it was challenging to adhere to societal norms in the early chapters of your life. But there's a difference now: you're armed with awareness. Back then, you may not have been fully cognizant of the extent to which you were conforming, as it seemed like the natural path. The authentic you, the version born complete and unadulterated, was overshadowed. Remember those days when you adhered to your parents' and society's dictates? Those days of following the rules? Well, it's time to shift your focus.

Your heart, your life, your essence. It's time to set your own rules, walk your own path and finally, unapologetically, give yourself permission to embrace your uniqueness, but this time, your keen awareness and self-assuredness will be your guiding lights as you navigate towards the real, unfiltered you. Numerous subtle ways go unnoticed, through which we fail to practice the art of saying yes to ourselves unapologetically. Yet, among these, a few standout behaviors that merit close observation include our unnecessary tendency to apologize, the inclination to overshare in an attempt to seem authentic and confident and the urge to offer explanations without being asked for them. These actions effectively impede our capacity to fully embrace our true selves without reservation. It's intriguing how this inclination to adhere to false niceties has become deeply entrenched within us. We often find ourselves plagued with feelings of guilt and remorse, even when our intentions or actions were not intended to cause harm or offense.

This pattern of conditioned behavior steers us towards carefully treading in order to avoid causing discomfort or pain. Ironically, this wariness often results in the very outcomes we strive to sidestep – the creation of misunderstandings and strained relationships. The price of our pretense is the corrosion of authenticity.

Nature thrives by being true to its intrinsic characteristics. The supposed "sin," if we can label it as such, lies in straying from life's innate flow. Going against the grain of our inner selves, which embodies our primal instincts, our raw emotions and our spiritual essence, constitutes a departure from our genuine nature. The profound beauty, however, rests in embracing every facet of our existence – the spotlight moments as well as the shadows, our hearts in all their complexity and our lives just as they unfold. The key is to celebrate ourselves exactly as we are.

Indeed, the ingrained habit of apologizing when it's unnecessary is something we often overlook. A prime example is when you invite someone into your home and find yourself apologizing for the clutter, the lack of picture-perfect tidiness; essentially, for not projecting an idealized image of yourself. It's as if we're attempting to preempt any judgment that might arise from the other person's perspective, but does the guest really care about your house being less than immaculate? Sure, they might have their own thoughts, but the truth is, their opinion holds little weight in the grand scheme of things. What really matters is your perception of your own space. Perhaps you've been postponing some cleaning and organizing tasks and that's absolutely fine. On the other hand, maybe you're entirely comfortable with the cozy chaos your home embodies.

Your home serves as a reflection of your inner world. A mirror to your inner sanctuary. The way you maintain your external environment often mirrors how you're feeling internally. Regardless of the scenario, it all comes down to your own feelings and thoughts about your living space. Accept both sides of the coin without judgment, whether it's the drive for cleanliness or the embrace of a bit of clutter. After all, it's your life, your space and your unique way of existing in the world.

There was a phase in my life where over-sharing became second nature to me. It felt like a normal part of who I was. I believed that through my excessive words, I could convey my intentions clearly and appear self-assured. Interestingly, from someone else's viewpoint, this tendency might have made me seem like an incessant talker or a know-it-all. And honestly, I find it somewhat amusing now. I've been labeled both and you know what? That's absolutely fine. How else are we supposed to learn and grow if we don't some-times stumble and make a spectacle of ourselves? In our pursuit of self-discovery and fulfillment, we sometimes embrace our inner fool. Even as I write this book, I notice that this habit occasion-ally resurfaces, but that's the essence of life; it's a continuous practice. Embedded within the word "practice" is the word "act." We are all actors in our own stories, yet paradoxically, we often seek others' validation and comprehension regarding the script of our lives.

Through observing my tendency to over-share, I've come to realize that intentions can speak louder in silence. What truly matters is what you genuinely feel and acknowledge within yourself. It's fascinating how each perspective holds a distinct hue, like a unique brushstroke in the collective canvas of existence. This diversity is the enchanting beauty of life, where our stories interweave, influencing us individually while shaping a grand tapestry of experiences. So, why not grant ourselves the liberty to stand unapologetically and confidently beneath our personal spotlight? It's a reminder that none of us are getting out of life alive. Embracing our uniqueness and radiating in our light seems like a fitting tribute to this fleeting journey we call life.

We've all found ourselves in those moments where the urge to explain ourselves takes over, maybe even to the point of over-explaining. It's a desire born from wanting to be truly understood or stemming from the fear of being misunderstood, leading to unnecessary and often tangled miscommunication. Paradoxically, even with all the effort we put into explaining, the result can still be confusion and misinterpretation. Perhaps the essence of life lies in a dance of contradiction, where we unlearn some of what we've been taught while blending in the wisdom passed down to us. The past has its significance, its place and its value, but the key difference comes from recognizing the value it holds for your own self. Ultimately, it's your perception that matters most (or matters least) when it comes to explaining. Sometimes, shedding the need to explain every detail can actually lead to clearer and more effective communication. The age-old saying "actions speak louder than words" may hold more truth than we think. Allowing our actions to authentically convey our emotions becomes paramount, but before we can express ourselves genuinely, we must first be conscious of our true feelings and intentions. This self-awareness liberates us from the fear of judgment and provides a foundation for unapologetic authenticity.

No one else should hold the power to determine your value or worth. You are not a creation of their making, so they don't possess the authority to dismantle you unless they physically end your life. That's a completely different narrative. Thus, the process of unlearning and reclaiming your life on your own terms becomes a proactive action. Recognizing that each of us is unique, shaped by our own stories and often molded by parental teachings, including the concept of explaining our every action, we begin to understand that our actions are an external manifestation of our internal world. It's a journey of becoming attuned, of being aware. Embracing the value of saying yes to yourself without any apologies, filters, or concern for the opinions of others is an undeniable truth. This authenticity holds a power that cannot be denied. If anyone attempts to persuade you otherwise, it's a cue to turn your focus inward, not in search of validation, but to reaffirm your self-worth and conviction. Remember, it's about being unapologetically you without the need for justification or approval from anyone else. It's as simple as that: a bold declaration of your own essence.

As we arrive at the close of this journey, a new saying comes to mind: "Life goes on." An apt encapsulation of life's unpredictable nature. Life unfolds, often devoid of predictability or conformity to our desires. Despite our yearning for things to align with our plans, each day ushers in moments as they are, offering us the choice to be genuinely present and attuned. The pivotal key to unlocking life's essence is awareness, yet, a curious paradox exists: many of us remain unaware of our awareness. We've internalized the art of suppressing our genuine selves, severing the connection to our inherent nature. In our quest to assign blame, we may point fingers at external influences such as society, parents, or companions for life's twists and turns, heartaches, or disappointments. However, in truth, the compass of responsibility points inward. Our experiences, choices and encounters are woven from the fabric of our unconscious decisions. Rather than imposing our expectations upon life and others, embracing the art of acceptance emerges as a transformative philosophy. Learning to embrace every facet of existence as it is, without preconceived notions, positions us to be in harmony with life's currents. This serene alignment grants us proximity to a life adorned with tranquility, elation and love. Yet, in this grand symphony of acceptance, there remains a crucial starting point: the journey of embracing oneself unapologetically! To claim the fullness of who we are, to offer unconditional acceptance to ourselves, sets the stage for the harmonious acceptance of life's intricate tapestry. As we embark on this profound introspection, let us shed the weight of self-judgment and the confines of imposed expectations. Let us traverse the realm of self-discovery, casting aside the illusions that shroud our true essence.

Life's anthem echoes the refrain of unyielding existence, portraying it as unpredictable, enigmatic and beautiful in its complexity. With each dawn, we're invited to dance in rhythm with life's cadence, free from the constraints of expectation. As we traverse this ever-shifting terrain, may we remember that the canvas of life holds splendor in its every brushstroke. By embracing ourselves wholeheartedly, we unlock the door to embracing life in all its breathtaking unpredictability, finding within it the serenity, joy and boundless love we've been seeking.

Many of us often assume that because we have settled into accepting things as they are, we have indeed embraced everything exactly as it stands. This perception can lead us to believe that we are genuinely content and fulfilled. However, have we truly delved into the authentic and profound acceptance of all aspects, encompassing everyone around us and, most importantly, ourselves? While it might seem effortless to embrace situations and individuals at face value, what about the intricate layers that lie beneath the surface? Are they not equally significant, if not more so? What defines us as a collective race? And, on a personal level, who are we? What force or influence shapes our identities? These questions hold a mirror to the very core of our existence, urging us to explore the intricate tapestry of our being. In our continuous journey of evolution and transformation, we find ourselves compelled to forge our path, guided by our unique principles. This path, however, is not devoid of inner conflicts. These conflicts often serve as catalysts for an intensified level of self-awareness, leading us to venture deeper into the labyrinth of our thoughts and emotions. As we navigate this complex voyage of existence, the revelations we unearth offer a profound realization: the surface acceptance we often settle for is, but a fragment of the greater whole. True fulfillment and self-discovery await those brave enough to dive into the depths of their authenticity. This process not only shapes our individual identities, but also contributes to the magnificent mosaic that defines humanity. In embracing the full spectrum of our emotions, experiences and relationships, we stand at the threshold of a higher state of consciousness, a state that transcends mere acceptance and blossoms into profound understanding and self-realization.

As I embarked on my SYTU journey, a mix of uncertainty and curiosity propelled me forward. I've always been drawn to uncharted territories and the pursuit of knowledge, so despite my apprehension, I embraced the challenge of delving into my inner world and viewing life through my unique lens. However, to put it differently, our current selves are the culmination of our past moments, representing a complex interplay of experiences that have molded us for survival. When someone wounded us in the past, that pain often follows us into the present, shaping our choices based on prior hurts. We often advocate for the mantra "let go and let God," yet in practice, we tend to hold onto past grievances rather than truly letting go. This erosion of trust extends not only to others, but also within ourselves.

This journey isn't about erasing the past; it's about understanding and integrating the memories and emotions that have shaped us. It's a process that requires embracing our narratives, those that have contributed to our present selves. In reality, this isn't a linear path of academic learning. It's more akin to life saying, "Remember those challenges I presented? Let's unpack them." However, it's not about rewriting history, but rather about channeling these experiences toward a brighter now and possible future.

It's a process of healing old wounds so they no longer impede our progress. "Trust the process" may sound like a platitude, but this is the journey where that phrase gains its true meaning. It's a journey, of reestablishing trust, acknowledging the scars that are part of our story while understanding that they don't define us. It's about renewing the trust we've lost, not only in others, but also in ourselves. Saying "yes" to yourself unapologetically might sound straightforward, but it's a practice that requires consistent effort. This journey is about more than a mere acknowledgment; it's a deep exploration of your essence.

Denial, often an emotional painkiller, loses its grip as you embrace vulnerability like a caterpillar in a cocoon; transformation occurs, shedding the old layers to reveal the authentic self that was always there.

The path to unapologetic self-acceptance doesn't demand justification. Your actions and choices are yours to make, not subject to others' judgments or expectations. This newfound autonomy is a gift we all possess, a privilege that reminds us of our intrinsic worth. When you unreservedly embrace your choices, you create a space for self-growth and transformation. In this journey, it's not just about saying "yes" to yourself, but about delving into the profound truth of your being. You are not defined by others' perspectives or societal standards. The cocoon of transformation you weave is a testament to your resilience and your commitment to unfold and emerge as your true self.

This process can be intricate, but each step is a testament to your evolution. So, as you navigate the intricacies of daily life, remember that saying "yes" to yourself extends beyond words; it's a practice rooted in self-love and authenticity. Your choices matter, your voice matters and your journey of self-acceptance paves the way for a life brimming with fulfillment and empowerment.

SAY YES TO U, UNAPOLOGETICALLY,
WITH NO FUCKS GIVEN!

Made in the USA
Las Vegas, NV
17 January 2024

84419864R00100